LOVE ME,
LOVE MY BROCCOLI

Other Avon Camelot Books by
Julie Anne Peters

HOW DO YOU SPELL GEEK?

LOVE ME, LOVE MY BROCCOLI

Julie Anne Peters

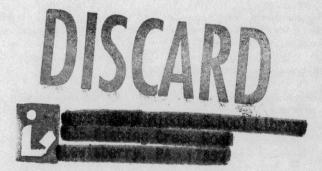

AN AVON CAMELOT BOOK

AVON BOOKS, INC.
1350 Avenue of the Americas
New York, New York 10019

Copyright © 1999 by Julie Anne Peters
Published by arrangement with the author
Visit our website at **http://www.AvonBooks.com**
Library of Congress Catalog Card Number: 98-93057
ISBN: 0-380-79899-9

First Avon Camelot Printing: February 1999

CAMELOT TRADEMARK REG. U.S. PAT. OFF. AND IN OTHER COUNTRIES, MARCA REGISTRADA, HECHO EN U.S.A.

Printed in the U.S.A.

OPM   10   9   8   7   6   5   4   3   2   1

To activists everywhere,
my respect and admiration

Chapter 1

Things that make me sick:
1. *Whitney what's-her-face and Paul Poole, kissing in public, especially in the cafeteria where others are trying to eat.*
2. *Meat. The smell of it, the sight of it, watching people eating it.*
3. *My mother—*

Chloe tensed. She slammed the cover on her mental journal and filed the last entry in her head under *To be continued.* "Later, if ever," she muttered.

"Hi, Chloe. Sorry I'm late. Mr. Keifer had a line of people waiting to talk to him, and I just had to get help with my biology assignment." Muriel Blevins plunked down her books and slid into the chair next to Chloe.

Chloe swallowed the soggy shred of lettuce that was gnashed between her teeth. She said to Muriel, "Since when do you need help with biology? You could probably give *him* a lesson on biomedical nuclear physics." She stabbed at a sunflower seed on her plate and added, "In your sleep."

Muriel sighed wistfully. She draped herself forward over her stack of books.

Oh no, Chloe groaned to herself. *Not again.* "Muriel, Mr. Keifer is ancient. I mean, he has to be fifty. Plus, he's bald and fat and probably married with kids our age. *Twice* our age."

"I don't care," Muriel said. "He's brilliant. We connected in class today, if you know what I mean. When our eyes met across the room, I sensed our brain waves modulating in sync."

"Oh, Mur. You're just having another out-of-mind experience."

She turned and scowled at Chloe. "What do you mean 'another?'"

Chloe widened her eyes at Muriel. "Remember Dr. Langstrom? As I vaguely recall, you were planning to quit school to become a Tibetan Sherpa so you could go with him on his yearly expeditions to Mount Everest."

Muriel shrugged. "I would have too, if it weren't for my acrophobia."

"You should've remembered you were afraid of heights before you prepackaged a hundred pounds of trail mix. And what about Mr. Holly, that math teacher you had last semester? You thought he was Jay Leno every time he said, 'So,

Muriel. What's your sign? Plus or minus? Heh heh.' " Chloe faked a gag.

"That was different. A childish infatuation. I was impressionable back then." Muriel picked up her can of guava juice, shook it, and peeled back the foil seal.

Watching Muriel guzzle down her guava, Chloe shook her head. "I'm glad Mr. Keifer gets your adrenalin going, kid," she said. "Now, we'd better get to work. Did you bring the flyers?"

With her free hand, Muriel slipped her notebook out from under her books. She flipped it open and handed a stack of pink pages to Chloe.

Chloe read the top sheet. "These look terrific, Mur."

Muriel finished her juice and set down the can. "You really think so?" She beamed at Chloe. "I'm not much of an artist. I didn't know if my computer graphics resembled the Brazilian macaw or not."

Is that what this is? Chloe studied the drawing more closely. She thought it was just a finger with a wart on it pointing to the text. Oh well, it was good of Muriel to volunteer to make the flyers. Believers were hard to find.

She scootched back her chair, stood up, and walked around the conference table, where the two of them had been lunching under their new club's banner. "Save the exotic birds of the world," Chloe called out in her commanding contralto. She thrust a flyer at a passing student, a girl she'd never seen before. "Halt the sale of exotic birds. Boycott all stores that sell birds of any kind."

The girl took the flyer, clucked in disgust, and dumped it in the trash with her lunch.

Undeterred, Chloe pressed a handful of flyers into a passing group of students. "Save our birds from the cruelty of black marketeers."

"What is this crap?" A hulking guy in sweatpants and a muscle shirt paused in front of the table. Squinting over Chloe's shoulder to read the banner behind her, he asked, "What's ARC?"

"Animal Rights Crusaders," Chloe explained. "We're working to protect and preserve the animal life on our planet."

"You mean like us?" He motioned to the group of guys who were clustering around him. "Us party animals?" They howled like hyenas. "And who are you supposed to be? Noah? Get it? Noah's arc?" He elbowed the guy next to him, who snorted.

Chloe's eyes narrowed. She punched a fist into her waist and said, "For your information, bucko, there are creatures on this earth who are suffering. Helpless creatures, sick and dying all because of human exploitation—"

"Who cares?" He crumpled the flyer and tossed it over Chloe's head.

Chloe felt the hot mercury rising up the thermometer of her neck.

The guy turned to his buddies and flapped his arms. "Arc, arc," he crowed. He swooped down with a claw finger and grabbed the beret off her head.

"Give it back!" Chloe's raspy voice rose to a shriek.

He took off across the cafeteria. Chloe charged after him.

"Chloe, forget it." Muriel caught up with her at the door. "Let him go. You have plenty of hats. Anyway, he's just a dumb jock and you know what they're like. Vapor between the ears." She demonstrated with puffed-out cheeks. "Plus, I think we've attracted enough attention." Muriel motioned with her chin to the growing, snickering crowd near the table.

Chloe flipped open her mental journal. *Things I hate, number four*, she etched in indelible think. *Jock Neanderthals.*

"This yours?" Chloe heard a deep voice behind her. She whirled. Her red felt beret dangled from the index finger of a hand. Instinctively her eyes traveled up the attached arm. She gulped. It wasn't just an arm. It was *his* arm. His deeply tanned arm.

"I apologize for that goon," he said as he fitted the hat back on Chloe's head. "You have to get used to Faber. He's a fullback. What do you expect?" He smiled at her.

Those eyes, she thought. *Those chocolate eyes. Stop it,* she chided herself. *He's one of them.*

"Backs are mostly muscle, especially from the neck up." He tilted his head down to meet Chloe's eyes. "That was a joke."

5

She straightened her shoulders. "Ha, ha," she said dryly.

He gave her a hurt puppy look. "Don't I even get a thanks for risking my life to rescue your hat from the hulk?" He hooked his fingers together in front and flexed.

Chloe sucked in a smile. She pivoted in place and mumbled, "Thanks." Then she hustled after Muriel toward the ARC table.

"You're Chloe Mankewicz, right?" he said behind her.

She stopped. Why was he following her? Even more important, how did he know her name? Chloe glanced over her shoulder and stared at him, then caught herself drooling and whipped her head back around. "Save the exotics," she called to no one in particular. Her voice had returned to its commanding throaty resonance.

"Mrs. Shilling was telling me about your club. She thought I might be interested in joining," he said at her side.

With nearly lethal force, she punched a fisted flyer into an unsuspecting pom-pom girl's stomach. When the girl doubled over, gasping for breath, Chloe mumbled, "Sorry." Why didn't he leave? Chloe wondered. She'd been about as rude as crude oil. She picked up her pace across the cafeteria.

"I guess because I wrote a paper on recycling, she thinks I'm out to save the world." When there was no response, he stepped in front of Chloe. "I'm Brett. Brett Ryan?"

She skidded to a stop, millimeters away from him. *I know who you are,* she replied to herself. All summer long she'd been watching him from her bedroom window while he mowed the neighbor's yard. Watching and wishing . . . She tried to dam the humiliating blush that was gushing into her cheeks. "So," she cleared her throat, "are you interested in joining, Brett Ryan?" She handed out a flyer to someone passing behind him.

He flinched and took a step backward. "Well, uh, no. Not really. Not that I think what you're doing isn't important. I mean, I do think we're trashing the earth. It's just that I have so much else going on right now. You know, football and wrestling, gymnastics coming up—"

"Well, you wouldn't want to bend over backward or anything."

He frowned.

She widened her eyes at him.

He burst into laughter.

He's laughing at me, she thought. Her anger flared again. Just as she was about to storm off, he punched her arm playfully and smiled. "Yeah, or flip out."

He touched me. Chloe melted in place. *Those eyes. That smile.* "I have work to do," she mumbled, ducking around him and away. Her clogs flapped to the meter of the time bomb in her head. "Save the exotic birds of the world," she bellowed, wincing as her voice cracked. "Boycott the grand opening of Bird Boutique this Saturday. We know for a fact they obtain their birds illegally through black marketeers. These merciless hunters sweep the forests for young birds, gas them, and tape their beaks. Then they transport them in crates for days or weeks on end without food or water. If the birds don't die of starvation, they die of despair. Don't allow this inhumanity to go on. Help save the birds."

She glanced back over her shoulder. Rats, he was gone.

Chapter 2

The front door was locked and the curtains drawn when Chloe got home from school. "Oh, great," she muttered. "What's Gran into now?" She rummaged around in her oversized tapestry bag for her keys.

Chloe unlocked the door. Warily, she pushed it in. The squeaky whine of the hinges dashed any hope she might have had for a surprise entry. She stuck in her head. "Gran?"

No response. A shadowy white shape appeared. "Hi, Deaf." She opened the door the rest of the way and stepped inside. Stooping to run her fingers along her sleek, white cat's arched back, Chloe surveyed the empty foyer. "Where is she?" Chloe whispered to her cat. "Where's Gran staked out today? Did guerrillas invade? Don't tell me, you didn't hear a thing." She smiled into the enraptured blue eyes of Deaf Leopard, her stone-deaf cat.

"Gran, where are you? It's Chloe," she called. No answer. She sighed and started up the stairs.

Without warning, the hall closet door flew open and a woman with a broomstick under her arm jumped out. "Hold it right there, assassin. One false move and you're a dead man."

Startled, Chloe stumbled on the steps. One clog fell off and she went sprawling. "Gran, it's me, Chloe," she said, rolling over and holding her hands up in the air. "Don't shoot!"

"Don't play mind games with me," the old woman seethed. "I know who you are . . . Ernst. Now, hand over that Luger nice and easy." She jabbed the stick at Chloe.

"Gran," Chloe pleaded, then sagged, realizing it was useless. Her grandmother's imaginary stint with the CIA had possessed her mind again. Chloe reached into her bag for the first thing she could find that might remotely resemble a Luger, whatever a Luger resembled. "Here." She held out a neon green highlighter to her grandmother.

"Put it down, right there. Reeeeal easy, Ernst." The old woman motioned with the broom handle to the bottom step.

Chloe set the highlighter up on end. In her best German accent, she said, "I sought vee ver rid of you een Berlin, Fraulein Mankevitz. But I zee you haf eluded our trap and outzmarted us again. I salute you." Chloe flicked stiff fingers off her forehead.

The woman's wrinkled lips pulled taut into an arrogant smile. "I know your tricks, Dmitri. Do you take me for a fool? You will never capture me, never. Now," she bent to sweep up the highlighter, "if you will excuse me, I have a plane to catch." She aimed the plastic pen at Chloe and dropped the broom. "Once again I slip through your fingers, assassin. Remember, I am the serpent." She hissed. Her beady eyes scanned the room. Then she backed up, crouched into the closet, and slammed the door behind her.

Deaf Leopard rubbed his cold nose against Chloe's cheekbone. "I thought I was Ernst," Chloe said to him. "Didn't she call me Ernst? If I was Dmitri I had the accent all wrong." She scratched behind his ear.

Deaf idled in a low purr. Chloe pushed herself up to her feet and counted to ten. Then she walked to the hall closet and knocked on the door. "Gran?"

"Chloe?" came the muffled reply.

Chloe smiled. She opened the door and held out a hand. Her grandmother blinked at her once before laying her frail fingers in Chloe's palm. "What am I doing in the hall closet?" she asked.

Tugging gently at her grandmother's elbow, Chloe replied, "You were, uh, cleaning out the coats to give to Goodwill." She shut the closet door behind her grandmother.

"Yes, of course." Gran patted Chloe's hand.

The cuckoo clock in the living room squawked four. "Is it that late? Your father will be home any minute and I haven't even started dinner. Now you go wash up. I'm making my Ukrainian specialty tonight to celebrate."

Oh no, Chloe thought. *Not again. Veal kotlety with brain sauce?* "Gran, remember I don't eat meat. . . ." She stopped. "Celebrate what?"

"Your birthday, of course. Your tenth birthday."

Chloe peered into her grandmother's glazed eyes. She reached up and hooked a loose tendril of gray hair behind the thin, translucent ear, and spoke tenderly. "Look at me, Gran. I'm almost fourteen now. My birthday's three months away. Remember?"

Her grandmother's eyes sparked momentarily, then died. "Yes, dear. Now go wash up. Get, get, get." She whisked Chloe away with the back of her hand. In her pink fuzzy slippers she shuffled off toward the kitchen, muttering, "Ten is such a trying age."

Chloe flung her beret Frisbee-style across the bedroom into the open cedar chest near her closet. She dropped her bag onto the bed, punched on the stereo, and hummed along with the soulful moan of a sax solo on KJAZ. Deaf took up his sentry position atop the vibrating speaker. On impulse, Chloe spun the dial until she hit a heavy metal rock station. Deaf yowled and leaped onto the bed. Cringing herself, Chloe declared, "You're right. It's deafening," and she turned the stereo off.

Chloe unfastened the black belt around her

waist and tossed it onto the bed. She'd redeemed it from a sale table last week at Janet's Near New. It wasn't easy to find nonleather belts—and for a quarter, what a steal. Chloe began to remove her blouse when she caught sight of herself in the full-length mirror.

"Yikes!" She covered her head. "Who says the wooly mammoth is extinct?" She picked up a wide-toothed comb from the bureau and yanked it through her shoulder-length curls.

"Maybe I should get a short cut like Mur's," she said to Deaf. "It makes her look so, I don't know, sophisticated. Is there such a thing as a 'chic nerd'? I don't think so. 'Chic geek?'"

Chloe twisted her unruly mop into a bun on top and secured it with extra-large bobby pins. "Better, Chloe. Now your head looks like a basket of Easter grass."

She exhaled audibly. *What could he possibly see in me?* she wondered. Aloud, she answered her own question, "A hideous new species evolving, of course. Sort of a cross between Jane of the Jungle and Alien Invasion. Forget it, Chloe. You're not his type. Not that you'd want to be, right? After all, he is one of *them.*"

She flopped on the bed. *Number five.* She flipped open her mental journal. *Hypocrites, especially one I know named Chloe Mankewicz.* She closed the journal. "Give it up, girl."

She stood and wandered toward the bay window. On her way she grabbed her Rhett Butler and Scarlett O'Hara dolls off the bookcase. Curl-

13

ing up on the window seat, Chloe pranced Rhett up to the crest of her bent knees. "Frankly my dear, I don't give a damn," she told him.

Liar. Chloe sighed and lowered the doll to her side. Her eyes strayed to the bookcase. It was getting a little crowded with *Gone With The Wind* memorabilia. And she thought Muriel was a hopeless romantic.

"So what?" Chloe countered aloud. She loved every piece of her collection. It had taken her years to scavenge all the treasures. At last count there were nine music boxes. Each one tinkled "Tara's Theme" in a slightly different key. She had an original movie poster, the one with Scarlett melting over Rhett's hot hands while Atlanta burned in the background; a third edition hardback by Margaret Mitchell, with most of the pages intact; and her newest addition, the two-set GWTW videotapes, last year's birthday present from Muriel, even though Muriel knew that Chloe didn't have a VCR. She didn't even have access to a TV. Chloe agreed with her father that TV was the root of society's decay, but she wouldn't mind watching GWTW just once more.

"Oh Rhett, Rhett," Chloe breathed in her thickest fake southern drawl. She glanced out the window to her neighbor's yard. "Take me, take me now. Brett, oh Brett—" She freaked. "What am I saying?" Mortified, Chloe threw Rhett Butler out the window.

Chapter 3

The "yowl" traveled up the trellis to Chloe's second-story bedroom window. She stuck her head out and cringed. Her father peered skyward, rubbing the growing welt on his head. "What are you playing?" he said. "*Gong* with the Wind?"

She made a face at him. "Sorry, Dad. Are you hurt?"

He examined his fingers. "I don't detect any *scarlett,* my dear."

Chloe rolled her eyes. "Guess you don't get blood with brain damage."

They exchanged sneers.

"Would you mind bringing my doll up on your way in?"

Dr. Mankewicz propped his bike against the rose trellis and bent to retrieve the Rhett Butler doll beside his foot. Chloe thought, not for the first time, that from a mile away you could guess that he was a college anthropology professor. Tall, handsome, wearing mismatched socks. Straightening, he adjusted his wire rims at Chloe. "Is Gran . . . ?" He let the question dangle.

"Cooking up her special Ukraine brain delight for dinner. My tenth birthday party, remember?"

He shook his head. Squinting up at her, he said, "I'm sorry, Chloe."

"It's okay. I'll just make a salad."

"Not about that. I forgot to buy you a present."

Chloe threatened him with the other doll.

He covered his head with his briefcase. "See you later. Oh, by the way—I'm taking up a new hobby."

"What? Dad!" Chloe's voice rose an octave, but he'd already disappeared through the patio door. "Oh, brother." She leaped to her feet. "What is it this time?"

"Your mother phoned me today at work." Chloe's father squeezed honey from the honeybear bottle onto his slice of pumpernickel bread. They were sitting across from each other at the dining-room table eating dinner. Chloe stopped chewing on a leaf of spinach momentarily, then began to gnash it mercilessly. "She wants you to call her," he said.

"In this life?" Chloe speared a cherry tomato and popped it into her mouth.

"Chloe . . ."

16

"Forget it, Dad."

"She wants to spend Thanksgiving with you."

Chloe choked. She grabbed her iced tea and took a swig. After she swallowed, she asked sarcastically, "What's she serving? Turkey with oyster stuffing? Giblet gravy? Baked ham? Or is she going to force me to stand by and witness brutal slaughter again when she plunges a live lobster into boiling water?"

He folded his bread in half. "She didn't realize it would upset you so much. She probably just forgot. Your mother understands that the two of you have philosophical differences."

"Understands? Dad, I still have nightmares about that lobster. It keeps flopping around helpless in those banded claws, trying to escape. She doesn't understand. How could she? She doesn't believe in anything."

"That's not true, Chloe. Just because she doesn't share your convictions," he met her eyes across the table, "doesn't mean she's amoral."

"No," Chloe muttered. "She's a moron."

He held her eyes. "Your intolerance is showing, my dear."

Chloe dropped her eyes. She felt the blood rushing to her cheeks. "But, Dad. She blinds bunnies."

He frowned at her.

Chloe shoveled another spinach leaf into her mouth. She hated that her mother worked for Desiree Cosmetics. Why couldn't she work for a

17

cruelty-free cosmetics company? Aveda or BWC? They never tested their products on animals.

There was a moment of silence while both Chloe and her father chewed and swallowed. Then Chloe's father, mopping up some gloplets of honey from his plate with the last crust of bread, said, "It could be worse. She could sell cars." He chomped on his bread and added, "On TV."

They both cracked up. Yes, she was definitely her father's daughter. Even though her parents had been divorced more than ten years, Chloe couldn't believe they'd ever been married. Or had a child. No way was she related to her mother.

Maybe I'm adopted, she thought. *Or cloned. Yes, that's it. I was a test-tube baby. And Mother just picked me up from the hospital. In her lavender Lexus with Desiree Cosmetics, Inc. plastered all over the back window.* Chloe shuddered.

She decided she'd better change the subject. "So, Dad, what's this new hobby of yours?"

"Ah." He wiped his mouth with a napkin. Behind his wire rims, his eyes twinkled. Rubbing his hands together, he leaned forward to speak. At that moment the dining-room lights went out. The door to the kitchen burst open and Gran shuffled in, carrying Chloe's birthday cake, all ten candles flickering in the dark.

"What time do you want to meet at Bird Boutique tomorrow?" Muriel asked. She shifted her stack of books from one arm to the other. "I have to be home by eleven for a dentist appointment.

Personally, I don't think that's enough time to demonstrate, especially for a cause as important as saving the exotic birds of the world. I'm going to ask Mom to reschedule for next Saturday."

"Good try, Mur." Chloe smiled. "You've already made her reschedule that appointment three times. You and your, what is it, ordontophobia?"

Muriel looked at her. "That's fear of teeth."

Chloe shrugged. "Close enough. What do you call the fear of fear itself?"

"Phobophobia." Muriel sneered and Chloe smirked.

Chloe scrounged around in her bag for the Bird Boutique grand opening announcement. They were standing at the street corner across from the middle school waiting for the traffic to clear. "Store opens at nine o'clock," Chloe read. "Let's meet at eight-thirty. I think two-and-a-half hours is a strong enough show of support." She started across ahead of Muriel. Over her shoulder, she asked, "You don't have some ridiculous fear of arrest, do you?"

"What?" Muriel's eyes bugged out. "Do you think we might get arrested? Chloe!" Muriel rushed up behind her, gouging the back of Chloe's arm with her metal ruler. "Do you really think there's a possibility?"

Checking her arm for blood, Chloe replied, "Don't worry, kid. If they haul us off to the slammer, I'll tell them you were my hostage. That's it, my psychological hostage. I'll tell them it was all my idea, that I threatened to expose you if you didn't cooperate."

Muriel exhaled a great sigh of relief. Then she frowned. "Expose me for what?"

"Lusting after a married man. That's got to be a crime."

"Chloe!"

Chloe burst into laughter and covered her head with her bag to soften Muriel's blow.

A swarm of students converged outside the front doors of the Aspen Grove Middle School. Along the sidewalk, a cluster of cheerleaders gathered—to swap beauty secrets, Chloe presumed. She and Muriel waved their way through the haze of perfume. Muriel's allergies kicked up and she started to cough. Chloe thought she'd have to write another scathing editorial to *The Aspen Grove Gazette,* this time about respecting people's rights to breathe fresh air. Maybe she'd throw in a few jabs at jocks while she was at it.

"Chloe, hi."

That voice. Chloe froze. She held the door open as he breezed past. "Thanks," Brett said, punching her arm. "If this is women's lib, I'm all for it." He smiled at her.

He touched me, she thought. She savored the tingle while several more people brushed by her unnoticed. *And he remembered my name.*

"Thanks, Chloe," someone said. "Bring the luggage in when you get a chance."

Like a sprung mousetrap, Chloe released the door. Unfortunately Muriel was waiting in the threshold, and the door smacked her in the jaw. The force hurtled her backward, right onto her rear.

"Mur, I'm sorry!" Chloe crouched to help her friend gather books off the floor. "Talk about vapor between the ears."

Muriel grinned. Without warning, she bolted to her feet. Chloe noticed the grin change to a sappy smile. "There he goes." Muriel sighed dreamily, gazing down the hall after Mr. Keifer. She absently took the books Chloe offered her and floated off on a cloud behind him.

"Oh, brother," Chloe muttered. She flung her bag over her shoulder and started down the hall in the opposite direction. "I hope I never act that stupid when I fall in love. Like I'm ever going to."

"What time's the big bird boycott?" Brett asked, suddenly appearing at her side.

Whoa, he was tall. And his sun-bleached hair shimmered in the fluorescent hall light. "The what?" Chloe asked. And he was always catching her off guard.

"The boycott tomorrow at Birdie Boutique. It's still on, isn't it?"

"Of course it's still on." She clucked. What did he think, she was all talk, no action? "We're forming the picket line at eight-thirty."

"Wow, you've got a whole picket line going?" He widened his eyes at her. "I'm impressed."

Uh-oh, she thought. *Did two a line make?*

"Do you always walk so fast? It's like warp

21

speed trying to stay up with you." He stepped in front of her and stopped dead.

Did he say I was warped? She felt a little tipsy, standing there close enough to feel his body heat. "What did you say?" She had to raise her voice over the growing din.

He nudged her sideways, out of the stampeding herd and against the lockers. "You're hard to talk to, you know that?" He propped his arm over her head. "And you never smile. You're so intense."

Chloe opened her mouth to retort, but she couldn't think of a retort, tart or otherwise. Luckily, the clanging bell overhead cut off all conversation.

"Oh, man." His eyes slid from hers to the watch on his wrist. "I'm late for practice." He backed away. He playfully boxed her arm and said, "I'll catch you later, Chloe. Tomorrow for sure. I want to talk to you about something."

He disappeared into the storm of students thundering down the hall. Chloe inhaled a deep, calming breath. She hadn't even exhaled it all when he reappeared.

Touching the tip of her three-cornered Paul Revere hat, he said, with a lopsided grin, "By the way, I like your hats."

Chloe smiled meekly.

He waggled a finger at her. "Hey, I did it. I made you smile."

She watched him sprint away until he had vanished around the corner. Then she spun in place and pounded her head on the locker behind her.

Chapter 4

Chloe was not about to let Saturday's weather put a damper on her day. Okay, so it was sleeting, it was freezing, it was gale-force winds. Chloe's stomach rivaled the worst tempest the Rocky Mountains could ever conjure up.

It was always this way before a demonstration or a sit-in, or any form of public activism. But today seemed worse. What did he want to talk to her about?

She pulled on her gabardine pants and began to tie the hip laces. Since this was going to be a stormy day at sea, she thought it fitting to wear her newest garage-sale acquisition, a genuine U.S. Navy uniform replete with sailor hat and tie. "Aye, aye, matey. Whar in thunder is that blimey parrot?" Chloe stuck an arm through the black wool peacoat. Deaf Leopard cocked his head at her funny. "You're right. I'm losing it."

Downstairs, she found her father in the dining room engrossed in a thick tome about the Incas. He glanced up. "You're still going, huh?" He took a swig of the hot herbal tea in front of him and added, "It's times like this I wish we had a car."

"For a few blocks in the rain?" Chloe scoffed. "Come on, Dad. We don't need to widen the hole in the ozone." She whipped her yellow poncho around her shoulders and zippered it up. Peering out the French doors at the inch of sleet that had collected in the birdbath out back, she shivered.

"Do you want me to go with you?" her father asked. "We could be the three picketeers."

"Sounds like a disgusting nose habit." Chloe curled her lip. She smiled at his chuckle, then crossed the room to kiss him on the cheek. "No thanks, but I appreciate the offer. Where's Gran this morning?"

"Sleeping in," he replied. "She was up again last night, prowling around for burglars."

"Spies, you mean."

His eyes dropped. He sighed wearily, turning to gaze out the patio doors. Chloe rested her cheek on top of his bristle-brush head.

"I asked Dr. Shaeffer how long the paranoia lasts," he said. "He told me it all depends on the person, and on the progression of the disease. Dementia or Alzheimer's, whatever it is, affects people in different ways, at different speeds. . . ."

"Don't worry, Dad," Chloe reassured him. "We

can take care of her. We have been for years. It's sad, but it's kind of funny, too." Chloe started to laugh. "Yesterday, when that new neighbor across the street drove up in his rusted-out camouflage van, Gran flew out the gate. She must have been picking up the last of the apples out back. Anyway, she ripped the stem off one and threw it at the van. Then she cried, 'Hit the dirt!' and scrambled behind the lilac bush, plugging her ears."

Her father burst into laughter. "Serves him right for driving that gas guzzler. It *was* blown to bits, I presume."

"Smithereens." Chloe gave his shoulders a firm pat. She headed toward the door. "I'll probably go down to the animal shelter after the boycott and work in receiving for a while. I should be home by three or four."

"I thought you were working adoptions at the shelter."

"Yeah, I was. . . ." Her eyes fastened on the front doorknob. "But, I, uh, kind of got fired. Not fired, exactly. Transferred."

"Why?"

She sighed and turned to face him. "I refused to adopt out some of the animals. I didn't think the people who wanted them would make very responsible owners. I mean, I thought that was part of my job—screening."

He frowned at her across the living room. "How many people did you screen out?"

She shrugged. "Everyone. But Dad . . ."

25

He started to laugh, then shook his head at her. "Chloe, you're a marshmallow." He removed his glasses to clean them with his handkerchief as his face sobered again. "I'm not real thrilled with you going back to receiving. All those abused and neglected animals coming in, I know it upsets you. I'd never ask you to quit, but promise me you'll think about it before you have a nervous breakdown. One mental case in the house at a time, please."

"You worry too much." Chloe reached for the doorknob. Sensing her father's lingering concern, she forced a cheery voice and said, "I have to do it, Dad. It's for the movement."

He sighed. "I know."

Muriel was huddled in the doorway of Bird Boutique when Chloe blew in. "Geesh," Chloe cried, bunching her rain slicker up around her neck. "This weather is for the birds."

"Literally." Muriel's teeth chattered as she bent to retrieve the picket signs. There were two of them, slats of cardboard stapled to wooden handles, leaning up against the wet brick building. "I have to warn you, Chloe," she said, "my brother trespassed in my room again yesterday and found the poster paints. One of these days I'm going to exterminate that little rodent."

"Let's see them, Mur." Chloe sacrificed a warm, dry hand from under her poncho.

Muriel, sniffling, flipped over one of the picket signs and thrust it at Chloe.

26

Chloe fought to contain her laughter. The signs were certainly colorful with all the little Mickey Mouses. That's what the drawings looked like to Chloe. She couldn't see any resemblance to a parrot or a cockatoo. It didn't matter. Against the battering of an October sleet storm, even the lettering on the posters was a runny, mucky mess.

Chloe blinked up into Muriel's beseeching eyes. "They look great, Mur. Anyway," she added quickly, "I think they'll attract attention, and really, that's our goal. Once people stop, we can tell them not to buy birds here. And I promise next week I'll do more. I already have the petition drawn up to send to the Department of the Interior asking them to officially declare the African elephant an endangered species."

Muriel blew her nose. "I'll do anything you need me to do, Chloe," she said. "You know that."

Chloe smiled warmly. Good ol' Mur.

For two hours they trooped back and forth on the slushy pavement outside Bird Boutique. The few people who braved the elements to attend the grand opening were greeted by a sniffly Muriel Blevins, who stuck out her tongue at each apathetic passerby, or a vocal Chloe Mankewicz, who yelled at their backs. They didn't deter many shoppers, although Chloe did manage to create a memorable impression on the scowling manager inside by referring to him frequently in her most resonant voice as "that bird butcher."

At ten forty-five Muriel's mother came to pick

her up for the dentist. "You want a ride to the shelter, Chloe?" Muriel asked.

"No thanks. I'll hang around a while longer. If I can save one more bird . . ." She sighed.

"You're so dedicated," Muriel said, squeezing Chloe's hand. "Isn't she dedicated, Mom?" Muriel smiled as she climbed into the car.

Chloe waved to the wet Toyota sputtering away. "Dedicated," she muttered, "Right." Between clenched teeth she seethed, "Where is he?"

She hated to admit it, but she would have left with Muriel if it hadn't been for *him*. He'd said he was coming, hadn't he? She'd busted a gut exhorting the inhumanities imposed on the bird world. And for what? For him? Of course not. She was here for the birds. Wasn't she? She believed in the cause. Didn't she?

A sports car honked as it zoomed by, sloshing water over Chloe's already soaked and frigid feet. "You dipstick!" she hollered after it. Where *was* he? Didn't he say he'd be here? Didn't he say he wanted to talk to her?

She caught sight of herself in the store window. "You're pathetic," she muttered. *Worse than Muriel. Worse than Scarlett, mooning over this prep jock.* Yanking her poncho up around her neck, Chloe exhaled in disgust and added, "Frankly, Brett, I don't give a damn." She tossed the pickets in a dumpster and stormed off.

She spotted him at lunch on Monday. Not that she was looking for him or anything. Not that her eyeballs ached after being glued to the cafeteria door for an hour. She'd rehearsed complete and total indifference in front of the mirror all weekend. She had it down. When he finally swaggered in, surrounded by admiring fans, Chloe launched into her act.

"Save the African elephant!" she cried. Ignoring his approach, she thrust her clipboard at a passing student.

"Oof," the guy grunted.

"Sorry," Chloe said. "Will you sign my petition?" she asked him.

The purple-haired punker held his ribs and scowled at her.

She said, "Are you aware that eighty thousand elephants are brutally slaughtered each year for their ivory?"

He staggered away.

She yelled after him, "Whole herds are poisoned. Or gunned down with machine guns. Adults, babies—"

"No kidding? Eighty thousand?"

Chloe whipped around, and gulped. "Two hundred and fifty slaughtered every day. And the hunters don't even wait for the elephants to die before they hack off their faces for the tusks." *What does he do, sprinkle Hershey's cocoa in his eyeballs at breakfast?* she wondered.

"That's unbelievable. Let me sign that." He extended his arm.

Chloe stared at the arm, then pushed the clipboard toward Brett. "If we can get the Department of the Interior to declare them an endangered species, it'll make hunting illegal. After that, we can start on the walrus poachers—"

"Could you help me with this letter I'm supposed to write to Governor Eicher? It's about the new gun control law and how kids are supporting it. Sort of like a petition, but I don't know how to do it."

So that was it. He needed a favor. "Sure," Chloe said. "Let me see it."

He smiled meekly. "I don't have it on me. I thought maybe we could get together later and work on it."

Get together? Her heart leaped. "Okay. When?"

He met her eyes. "How about Friday night?"

Friday. Night, Chloe repeated to herself. That sounded late. Like a date. "Where?" she asked.

"The new mall."

"Huh?"

He cleared his throat. "I thought maybe we could talk about it over, you know, something to eat." His Adam's apple bobbed. He crossed both t's in his name with a swooping stroke and handed the petition back to Chloe.

I must be hallucinating, she thought. *Did he say something to eat, as in dinner, Friday night?*

"Well?"

She scraped her chin off the floor. "Sure. Okay."

"Yeah? All right." He tilted his head and squinted into her eyes. "I can't figure you out,

Chloe Mankewicz. You're . . . you're different. Interesting."

Weird, strange—she added her choice of adjectives. To him, she said, "Wait until you see my hair, if you want different, interesting."

He laughed. Reaching across to touch a stray curl on her shoulder, he asked, "What's wrong with your hair?"

"Careful." She recoiled. "You could lose a finger in there. I breed tarantulas for lunch money."

He laughed again. "You crack me up. Is that why you always wear hats, to cover your hair?"

Chloe felt the blood gush into her cheeks. "No." She lowered her eyes. "I just like hats."

He lifted the black netting from the top of her green pillbox and brought it down over her eyes. Leaning close, he whispered through it, "I think this one is *very* cool."

Hokay. Chloe stepped, almost fell, backward as she caught her breath and yanked up the net. *Can he hear my heart pounding?* she wondered. *The whole* school *can hear your heart pounding, you idiot. They must think we're having an earthquake.*

"Friday," he said. "I'll pick you up at six. Maybe afterwards we can do a flick. Yeah, Italian and a flick. Oh, and Chloe. Wear that hat, okay?"

After I bronze it and hang it in the Smithsonian? she thought. "Six," she said.

Without warning, Muriel spun Chloe around by the arm. "He signed it, Chloe," she breathed. "Look, Mr. Keifer signed the petition." Muriel showed her, then hugged the clipboard to her chest, sighing wistfully.

"Keifer. Biology," Chloe repeated, her eyes following Brett as he sauntered away toward the hot-lunch line.

"Was that Brett Ryan you were talking to?" Muriel touched Earth base again. "Remember when you said he probably uses a tire pump to inflate the space between his ears?" She snickered.

Chloe freaked. Dropping her clipboard and grabbing Muriel by the shoulders, she cried, "What does 'do Italian' mean? Do Italian and a flick, what does that mean, Muriel?"

Chapter 5

"I know you think I'm nuts, Mur." Chloe zipped her crushed velvet dress, circa 1940, up the side. "I can't believe it myself. Why did I say yes to him?" In the mirror she smoothed the crumpled lace bodice over her protruding shoulder blades.

"I don't think you're insane, exactly." Muriel opened one of Chloe's GWTW music boxes to unleash a tinkling strain of "Tara's Theme" into the bedroom. "It just surprises me, that's all."

Stepping into red silk pumps, half a size too big, Chloe turned to pose in front of Muriel. "Does this look stupid? Tell me the truth. Do I remind you more of Dorothy or Toto?"

Muriel prattled on, "I mean, I thought we agreed that jocks were bicep brains. We always pictured ourselves marrying older men, distinguished men, men of class. I didn't think the eighth-grade class counted."

"For heaven's sake, Mur," Chloe turned away from her. "He just wants help with a letter." So why did it feel like a date? *A ten-second date if I show up looking like this.* She groaned. "The green pillbox is hideous with this dress. I look like the ghost of Christmas past." Chloe shuddered.

Now Muriel giggled. Quickly she covered her mouth as Chloe shot her dead with eye daggers. Lowering herself onto the bay window seat, Muriel said with a sigh, "You're right, Chloe. I guess I'm just jealous." She rested her elbows on her knees. "My last date, my only date, if you'll recall, was with that guy Harold. Remember? My mom's college roommate's son. She made me take him to the church's New Year's Eve dance when they came to visit over Christmas last year. I was never so humiliated in all my life. He had that bleached-blonde mohawk and leather pants so tight you could see . . . well, I won't be graphic. He only came up to here on me," she sat up and stiff-armed her chest, "and every time we danced a slow dance—"

"That's why they call male pigs swine," Chloe cut her off. "What do you think about this?" She twirled in front of the mirror. Chloe thrust out her arms, palms up, for Muriel's appraisal.

Muriel gasped and jumped to her feet. "It's exquisite, Chloe. You've never worn that jacket before. Is it silk?" She rushed over to stroke it. "The

fire-breathing dragon embroidered on the back"—
she spun Chloe around—"it's absolutely exotic."

"I hope it doesn't give him any ideas," Chloe
muttered. She pulled on the matching emerald-
green slit skirt while explaining to Muriel, "My
mother bought this outfit for me in Chinatown
last time she was in San Francisco, at one of her
Desiree Cosmetics rah-rah rallies. I thought I'd
donated it to Goodwill, like everything else she
ever gave me." She half turned in the mirror to
view the back. Then, fitting the pillbox onto her
head, she stared at her reflection. "Why do I have
this sudden urge for an egg roll?" Chloe's stomach lurched. "Hooboy. I think I feel the Asian flu
coming on."

Italian turned out to be pizza, the flick was
a movie, and the surprise was that they were
doubling—with Turk and Alyssya, two y's.

The second surprise was that Brett's brother
Kenny was driving.

"Guys, this is Chloe." Brett made the
introductions.

Turk and Alyssya sort of grunted from the
backseat of the car where their lips were fused.
In front, Brett's brother turned around and gave
Chloe the once over.

Chloe forced a smile.

"You look awesome," Brett told her, sliding in
beside her in the backseat. "You remembered to
wear my favorite hat."

"I, uh, grabbed it at the last minute," she said,

adding to herself, *from its flashing pedestal on my dresser.*

Brett slammed the door. The lump beside her moaned. She couldn't help wondering if they were ever coming up for air. *Careful,* she thought. *You can drown in the sea of love.*

"Chloe?"

"What?" She blinked back to Brett. "I'm sorry. Did you say something?"

Brett tilted his head at her and arched an eyebrow. "I said, what do you think of Kenny's new Chev?"

"His Chev?" Brett's brother's face looked pretty smooth to her. No noticeable nicks.

"The H-rod."

"The what?" Her eyes widened.

"His Z28. Camaro." No response. "The car?"

"Oh, the car. It's, uh . . ." She was at a loss for words.

"Cool, huh?"

She was thinking it was warm. Really warm. She wondered why they all had to be crammed in the back. Then she saw that there were bucket seats up front. She could be sitting in Brett's lap. Never mind.

Chloe leaned forward and peered into the instrument panel. "What's your EPA?" she asked Kenny.

"Huh?" he grunted.

Brett laughed.

"What?" she asked innocently.

"Well, most girls ask if the tape deck works, does it have a CD player, how fast does it go out."

Chloe shrugged, wondering, *how fast does* what *go out?* "Guess I'm not most girls."

Brett smiled. "Guess not." To Kenny, he added, "See, I told you she was different."

Chloe swore she heard Kenny mumble, "Geek," but she couldn't be sure over the roar of the engine as they pealed out.

While they tooled along, at just under Mach two by Chloe's calculation, Brett informed her, "It's all Naugahyde upholstery. Port-injected, five liter, V8. Chrome bumpers, custom paint, Bose stereo . . ."

Chloe just smiled. He was so gorgeous.

When they got to the mall, Kenny dropped them off at the Pizza Alley across from the theater. "I'll be here at nine-thirty, sharp," he said. "If you're not, you walk." The car spewed gravel as it ripped away from the curb.

We might live longer if we walked, Chloe thought.

It took about two minutes for Chloe to figure out that Brett's best friend Turk was a toad. Explaining about her vegetarianism had never been a problem before, except maybe to her mother, who treated it like an eating disorder. But Turk had a royal conniption.

"I ain't eating no veggie pizza," he said. "Barf-a-roach. Let's get our regular, the Rocky Mountain of meat." Alyssya batted ten-pound eyelashes up at him, maintaining a symbiotic relationship with his arm.

Chloe glowered at them. "Do you realize the meat in this place probably comes from a farm factory? You do know what a farm factory is?"

She studied their vacant expressions. *Why do I talk to air?* she wondered. "A farm factory is where they breed the animals you eat for food. Are you aware of the cruel conditions these poor creatures are forced to endure so you can have ground-up flesh for *your* Rocky Mountain of meat?"

Not a blink. She shook her head. "Obviously not. Well, let me educate you. First of all, the animals are fed chemically-treated grain and steroids to fatten them up, so fat most of them can't even stand. Then they're shot full of antibiotics because the meat is so diseased. . . ."

Alyssya gasped. Turk groaned, "Geezus, you're making me puke."

Chloe grinned. For Alyssya's benefit, she added, "Most of the farm animals are murdered before the ripe old age of one. That's because babies are more tender, you know."

Alyssya's eyes welled with tears. Brett squirmed uncomfortably. "Why don't we order a medium veggie and a medium Mountain," he said. "That okay with you, Chloe?"

She shrugged.

"Turk?"

He grunted. Alyssya blew her nose in a napkin.

"Oh, now *that's* appetizing," Chloe muttered.

Brett glanced sideways at her, unsuccessfully attempting to stifle a grin.

Chloe twisted to face Brett. "So where's this letter?"

He pulled out a folded sheet of paper from his letter jacket pocket and handed it to Chloe. She read it. It was awful. *The governor will have to put off the gun control bill indefinitely until more money could be allocated toward education,* she thought.

"It's pretty bad," Brett said.

"No," Chloe lied. "It just needs a little editing." She flicked her Bic. It needed a total rewrite.

After she finished scribbling all over the letter, she handed it back to Brett, and said, "I'll be glad to get signatures for you if you want. Since we're gathering them for our petition anyway."

"Yeah? Great. Thanks." He read her revisions and smiled. "I really appreciate this, Chloe." He refolded the letter, stuck it in his jacket, and reached across to take her hand.

Chloe didn't hear much else of what went on. She was totally tuned in to Brett's hand squeezing hers. While he talked, his fingers flexed, sending a trill of tingles up her arm every single time.

When the pizzas arrived, Turk glared across the table at Chloe, and said, "Aren't you even going to take your hat off to eat? Or don't vegematics got any manners? Maybe you're afraid we'll see the potatoes sprouting on your head. Get it? Potato head?" He cracked himself up. Alyssya covered her lips with her fingers and tittered.

Before Chloe's foot reached Turk's shin, Brett snapped, "Shut up, dog breath." He released Chloe's hand and pulled the netting down over her eyes. "Don't give Chloe any grief about her hat. I love this hat." He smiled.

Chloe wondered, *Are those stars I see? Or just sparkles in the ceiling plaster?* When Brett added, "Hand over a piece of that veggie pizza for me, will ya?" Chloe answered her own question. I do believe it's the Ryan Constellation.

Chapter 6

The flick was called *Dirty Double Cross,* a blood-and-guts shoot-em-up with a cast of shadowy figures. There was a demolition derby every two, three minutes—whenever the plot dragged. Chloe had the mystery figured out about ten minutes into the movie. She guessed that the slinky blonde was the dirty double crosser. Boring, predictable. Chloe felt more heart palpitations opening the front door at home every day wondering where Gran's head had tripped off to.

Next to her Brett watched, entranced. During one particularly intense scene, which Chloe almost missed through a yawn, she heard Alyssya scream. Chloe muttered, not too quietly, "She must have just realized that Turk is short for Turkey."

Brett silenced Chloe with a vise-like grip on her hand.

The front-porch light was on at Chloe's house when they pulled into the driveway. As Brett walked her to the door, Chloe had a sudden foreboding; what if Gran was lurking in the lilac bush, wielding a zucchini Uzi or an apple grenade? Chloe leaned over the wrought-iron railing on the porch and spread the branches. She peered into the thicket.

"What are you doing?" Brett asked.

Chloe spun around. "Just, uh, thought I saw something move." She smiled at him. "We've had this snake problem."

Brett gave her a funny look. Then he took a step toward her. *What's he doing?* she wondered. He put his hands on her shoulders. *Oh, no. I'm not ready for this.* She braced. He smiled into her eyes. She licked her lips.

He turned her around so that her back was facing him. *What am I worried about?* she wondered. *He's just going to shove me in the door and run.* Instead, he said, "I love your clothes." His finger traced the outline of the dragon down the entire length of her back.

"Thanks," she croaked, breathing more fire than the dragon.

In a sweeping move, he turned her around and kissed her. For a moment. For a lifetime.

"Can I call you?" he asked afterwards.

Chloe, still comatose, nodded automatically. She said, "My number's—"

"I know your number."

*   *   *

42

"I know your number," she repeated in bed, lowering her voice to imitate his. "Eeeoooh!" she squealed, pulling her giant stuffed panda over her head. Deaf made railroad tracks in the quilt as he slid off the panda to the floor.

The next morning Chloe was awakened from her blissful dream by a muffled knocking on the bedroom door. Next to her, Deaf mewled and burrowed in closer.

"Chloe? You have a phone call," her father's voice floated in from the hall.

"Yes!" She threw back the covers. She leaped out of bed, while Deaf clung to the panda for dear life. In a single bound, Chloe unhooked her robe from the back of the door, yanked the door open, and parachuted down the stairs.

"Thanks, Dad," she said breathlessly, holding the phone to her hammering heart. She inhaled deeply once, twice. "You can go now, Dad." She widened her eyes at him.

"Oh, uh, right." He cleared his throat as if he wanted to say something. Then, apparently changing his mind, he clamped his jaw shut and scuttled off to the dining room.

What's with him? Chloe wondered. She shrugged it off. A case of parental weirdness. After another deep breath, she held the phone up to her ear. "Hello?" she said in her most casual voice. *Do I sound hysterical?* she asked herself.

"Hello, darling."

Like a scud missile, Chloe's heart crashed through the linoleum. "Hello, Mother," she said.

"How are you, darling? I haven't heard from you in ages. Did your father tell you I called? I know how absentminded he can be. Since you didn't return my call—"

"He told me." Chloe wrapped her robe tighter around her. She knotted the belt to ward off the sudden chill in the air. "I've just been busy lately."

"I see," her mother said coolly. "What are you doing this evening? I thought we might have dinner together."

"What about Roger?" Roger was her mother's boyfriend, an aerobics instructor at her health club. Chloe stuck out her tongue. *Gag me with a leotard.*

When she answered, the hint of a southern drawl underscored her mother's words, even though she hadn't lived in Louisiana for twenty years. "Roger is in New York on business. If you'd like we could see a movie together. I hear that new suspense thriller, *Dirty Double Cross,* is wonderful."

Chloe rolled her eyes. *Roger's out of town, so you have time for me, is that it? What about all those times I needed you? All those years you were too busy with your career, or your latest boyfriend, or blinding bunnies to think about spending time with me?* "I can't, Mother. I'm busy tonight. Besides, I've already seen the movie and it's boring."

Another uncomfortable pause. "What are you busy with?" she asked.

None of your business, Chloe flared inwardly.

She held her tongue, literally, between her teeth. "I'm going out." *Oh, boy, why did I say that? Now she'll hound me for details.*

"You mean on a date?"

Chloe clenched her teeth. "Don't sound so shocked, Mother. Stranger things have happened." Chloe hesitated. "Okay, so I can't think of any at the moment. . . ."

Her mother laughed. "Forgive me, darling. It just never crossed my mind that you might have a date. But then, you are almost fourteen now, aren't you? If anyone asks, we're sisters."

"Right," Chloe said. Her mother's idea of a joke, though Chloe knew it wasn't. Not really. *Here's where I'm supposed to tell her she doesn't look a day over thirty.* "Thirty centuries," Chloe mumbled.

"What was that, dear?"

"Nothing." Chloe clamped her jaw.

Her mother sighed. "I suppose you do have a full social calendar now that you're dating."

Chloe cringed. *I'd better get us off this subject.* "Yes, Mother, I'm not lying to you. I really am busy. This afternoon I'm demonstrating against prison camps for animals at the opening performance of Circus Kiev. Then, next week the Humane Society is coming to the school to let people know they have a right to refuse to dissect animals in the biology labs. They asked me to give a speech, so I'll be working on that tomorrow. Also, my new organization, Animal Rights Crusaders, is antivivisection, of course. We're doing a campaign to promote cruelty-free products. Desiree Cosmetics, by the way, are *still* being tested on animals."

"Yes, I know, Chloe. You don't need to keep reminding me." Her mother's accent thickened noticeably.

Chloe licked her index finger and added another marker to her bingo board.

"You are a busy person." Her mother sighed again. "I don't suppose your father mentioned my invitation for Thanksgiving?"

"That's ages away, Mother. Why don't we discuss it later?"

"Because it won't happen," she snapped. "You'll avoid discussing it with me, like you've developed quite a little habit of doing. I'd like to have your answer now so I can make plans."

Chloe felt trapped. She could tell her mother she didn't care if she ever saw her again, but that would be heartless. Besides, it wasn't the truth. At least, not the whole truth. She could never confide in her that Thanksgiving had become the saddest day of her life, that she mourned all the millions of turkeys bred in cruel conditions just to be slaughtered for one lousy dinner. Her mother would never understand. Anyone who could drop a live lobster into boiling water could hardly be expected to sympathize with a turkey.

"I hate to leave Dad alone with Gran," she settled on. "You know how she is."

Her mother said, "Why don't I ask them both to come along? Then you won't have any excuse."

Chloe blanched. Was it her imagination, or did she hear her mother mark her own bingo card? Chloe muttered, "I guess that'll work."

"Wonderful. I'll plan on it. Now, I want to hear all about your date."

Chloe choked. "I'm already late for my ARC meeting with Muriel. It was nothing, anyway. Just a movie. No big deal." *Right. So why am I dying inside?* she wondered.

Chloe's mother said, "I'll call you later in the week, darling. We can talk about it then. Maybe you can fit me into your schedule for say, a quick bite of dinner? Vegetarians do eat sometime, don't they?"

Chloe flared again. *That's right, Mother. Bash me at every opportunity.* "We eat, when the grazing's good," she said.

"I know a fabulous salad bar. We'll go there."

"Fabulous."

Apparently, her mother caught the sarcasm and cut the conversation short. After she hung up, Chloe exercised her jaws. They ached from clenching her teeth so hard. Deaf appeared, rubbing against her ankles and purring like a motorboat. Chloe bent to pick him up. She flopped him over her shoulder and padded to the sink to fill the teapot. Just as she set it on the stove to heat and was heading back upstairs with Deaf, the phone rang again.

"What does she want now?" Chloe grumbled. "She always has to call back with the vital trivia she forgot." She held Deaf out in front of her.

" 'Oh, by the way, dear,' " she mimicked her mother's voice. " 'Mary Beth Bellingham was telling me that her daughter Trysha—you remember Trysha, with a y? That sweet little neighbor girl you used to eat mud with?—well, she's prom queen of the universe this year, blah, blah, blah . . .' " Deaf scraped a sandpaper tongue across the tip of Chloe's nose. She kissed him back. She lowered him to the counter and picked up the phone.

"Yes, Mother." Chloe folded her arms in resignation as she rolled her eyes at Deaf. "What'd you forget?"

"I'm going to have to get a voice-change operation if I sound like your mother," a male voice said.

Chapter 7

Chloe dropped the phone. It landed with a thud and bounced across the kitchen floor. She gasped, fell to her knees, and hauled it back in by the cord. "Are you still there?" she asked, juggling the receiver up to her ear.

"Are we having an earthquake and nobody told me?" Brett asked.

Chloe giggled. She leaned up against the dishwasher to sit cross-legged on the linoleum. "No earthquake." *Except in my stomach,* she thought. "Sorry."

After a short pause, he said, "You want to go to the football game with me today?"

Chloe hesitated. *Should I tell him the truth?* she wondered. *Come on, Chloe. 'Fess up. Tell him you despise football.*

"The game's at two between us and Laguna.

Kelso's got a groin pull so he can't play, and I'm the backup quarterback. It's my big chance. I thought you might like to come watch me dazzle the high-school scouts." He gave a short laugh. "Or destroy all hope of me ever getting on the team."

"Football, huh?" she repeated.

"Afterwards, I thought we could hang a while at Cal's Tex Mex. You know, the dive where everyone meets after the games? 'Course, depending on how I do, you may not want to be seen with me in public."

She couldn't imagine that. Ever. "Sounds like fun," she said. "The afterwards part, anyway. I don't really want to go to the game, Brett. I mean, alone. If you're playing, I'd have to sit alone, right?"

"Turk plays tight end—"

Figures, Chloe thought.

"—so I'm sure Alyssya'll be going. You could sit with her."

Like I said, I don't want to be alone. Chloe had a thought. "Would you mind if I invited a friend?"

He paused. "Girl, I hope."

Was he jealous? Chloe clucked. *Get real.* "Android, actually," she replied. "She's programmed to follow me anywhere."

"Translation?"

Chloe smiled. "My best friend, Muriel."

"Oh, sure. That'd be cool. She can bring her boyfriend too, if she wants."

Chloe said to herself, *I'll tell Muriel to dig up*

Harold's number. "She isn't really going out with anyone right now," she told Brett, adding to herself, *unless you count lusting after Mr. Keifer.*

"Want me to fix her up? There are always a few guys on the team in-between girlfriends."

Chloe asked, "Is that what you are, in-between girlfriends?"

"Not anymore."

Chloe's ear melted all over the receiver.

"What does your friend look like?" he asked.

Oh, you know. Your basic nerd. "Well, she's really smart. An honor student, and just about the nicest person—"

"Maybe I'd better not, Chloe," he cut her off. "I wouldn't want it to come between us. I mean, it's not easy matching people up, you know? If they didn't get along, they might wreck our time together. Then later they'd blame us for ruining their reputations or some other head trip."

"Whoa, we wouldn't want to cause permanent psychological damage," Chloe said sarcastically. She added quickly, "That's okay, Brett. It was nice of you to think of her. Muriel can still come with me to the game, can't she?"

"Oh, sure," he said. "Then if we want to be alone later," he lowered his voice, "and I'm sure we will . . . we can drop her off. Okay?"

Something in that plan didn't sit right with Chloe, but she couldn't say what. Might have been her hyperventilating that was making her light-headed. Anyway, she was new to this dating game, so maybe that was the way it was played.

*   *   *

"The kickoff's at two, Muriel." Chloe cradled the phone on her shoulder while she poured herself a cup of chamomile tea at the stove. "I'm sorry to cancel our protest march at Circus Kiev, but this came up, you know, unexpectedly. Please say you'll go with me."

"Of course I'll go with you," Muriel said. "Even though I don't understand this. I don't understand you. I thought we agreed football was strictly for anthropoids."

"It is," Chloe replied. "And most of them are apes, I grant you. Except for Brett. I mean, he's a real person, even if he is a jock. I want you to meet him, Mur. Tell me if I'm being a hypocrite to go out with him."

Tell me why I completely lose control of my senses whenever I'm around this guy.

"Muriel," she slid down the side of the stove and onto the floor, "tell me if I'm acting like a ditz. On second thought, don't."

The football game was worse than boring; it was brutal. Chloe watched through her fingers, cringing every time she heard the crunch of bones or the crack of helmets. Whenever Brett got sacked, which was way too often for Chloe, she felt certain he was dead. At this rate, she figured, he'd be lucky to come away with less than a full body cast.

Muriel brought along her biology homework.

"What's the difference between meiosis and mitosis?" she asked.

"Oof. Did you see that, Muriel? That primate just punched Brett in the stomach. I hope his paw swells up." Chloe leaped to her feet. "Kill 'em, you baboons!" she bellowed.

"I've never known you to get so involved in blood sports," Muriel remarked, glancing up from her notebook. "I take that back. You were pretty loud last summer at the prairie-dog shoot."

"Barbarians." Chloe plopped down on the bleachers, shaking her head. She turned to Muriel. "How could a rational human being ever justify shooting defenseless prairie dogs for sport? Or any other animal, for that matter?" Out of the corner of her eye, she saw Brett get tackled from behind. She jumped up and screamed, "Mow that turfhead down!" Chloe plopped back down.

Muriel frowned at her. Chloe chewed a knuckle.

At Cal's Tex Mex after the game, Chloe and Muriel each ordered a bean burrito, while Brett and the rest of the team ate six or eight hundred tacos. Chloe lost count.

"Heck of a game, Ryan." Someone slapped him on the back. "That quarterback sneak was awesome. Super rollout to Penney. Keep playing like that and Kelso's gonna have to win his position back."

"Thanks, McCaffrey," Brett said, beaming. "Hey, I want you to meet my girlfriend, Chloe. Chloe, this is Lance McCaffrey. You've probably heard of him. He's the junior state recordholder in the freestyle. McCaffrey, Chloe."

"Hi," Chloe said absently. Her mind replayed the introduction. Did he say girlfriend? What's a freestyle? Could she get one for her hair? Where?

"And this is Chloe's friend, uh . . ."

"Muriel," Chloe rescued him. They all stared at Muriel, who was punching numbers into her scientific calculator at megahertz speed. Chloe elbowed her. Muriel whipped her head up and blinked. "Is it time to go?"

Chloe blanched. "Muriel says hi."

Brett introduced Chloe to all his friends: Tad Underhall, right guard. A deodorant? Fullenwider, catcher. Of what? KC Tall, at short. It was all pretty confusing. Chloe didn't know much about sports. The only thing she felt sure of was the thrill of victory every time Brett said, "This is my girlfriend, Chloe."

After the crowd at Cal's broke up, Brett and Chloe walked Muriel home. More like ran her home. As Brett yanked Chloe away from Muriel's door, she yelled over her shoulder, "I'll call you later, Mur."

"Chloe, would you mind if I asked you something?" Brett said when they were alone, walking back toward Chloe's house.

Is this when he proposes? she wondered. "I do," she said. Did I say that? "I mean, go ahead." She felt her cheeks growing pink.

"I don't want to hurt your feelings or anything, but . . . well, your friend's kind of a geek."

Chloe laughed. "I know. It's her most endearing quality."

Brett answered with a lopsided grin, "I don't know about that. I was going to ask you not to bring her along next time. I mean, she doesn't fit in, Chloe. She makes me, you know, uncomfortable."

Chloe felt her anger rising like a candy thermometer up her neck. Brett squeezed her hand. "I did hurt your feelings. I'm sorry. I just wanted you to know how I felt. There shouldn't be any secrets between us, not if we're going to start going together."

The mercury slid back into its reservoir. "Are we?"

He smiled at her. "Aren't we?" That smile.

"Look, about Muriel—"

"It's probably the same way you feel about Turk," he said. "I know you think he's a goon, but we've been friends a long time. I guess I see things in him other people don't. We've been through a lot together, me and Turk. Anyway, I don't plan to force him on you every time we go out. Maybe once in a while you wouldn't mind doubling, but that's up to you. Same with Muriel." He cocked his head at her. "That okay?"

How could he be any more reasonable than that? Chloe wondered. He was right about Turk. The guy was gutter sludge. She detested him. But Brett couldn't possibly feel the same way about Muriel, could he?

She cast her eyes up at him, and he smiled

back. She nodded agreement, and he leaned down to kiss her. It was their first mutual understanding.

"Look at that!" Chloe cried suddenly, her head whipping around. Eyes narrowed, she stared across the lane of cars stopped at the traffic light. "Can you believe that idiot? Wait here."

Chapter 8

Chloe charged across two lanes of traffic, zeroing in on her target. She marched up behind a crusty Ford pickup to the driver's side window and rapped on the glass with a white-knuckled fist.

The startled driver rolled down his window. "What the . . ." he sputtered.

Chloe glared at him. "Do you know how many dogs are injured or killed every year because their owners allow them to ride in open-bed vehicles?"

"Huh? What are you talking about?" He flicked a cigarette butt over Chloe's head.

"Your dog." She pointed to the panting German Shepherd behind her. "Don't you know how irresponsible it is to let your dog ride in the back? What if you have to stop suddenly? What if he decides to jump out in the middle of traffic? Don't you care about your animal's safety?"

"Get lost," he snarled, rolling up the window.

Chloe pressed her fingers down over the rim of the glass. "Look, mister," she said. "You may not care about your dog, but there are people who do. I'd be glad to take him off your hands and find him a responsible owner."

"Come on, Chloe. Leave him alone." Brett was beside her, pulling her wrists away from the window. With a final wrench of the handle, the driver sealed the window shut.

"Brett, he's going to kill that dog." Chloe's voice rose in anger.

"It's his business," Brett said. His fingers clamped firmly around her arm as he began to lead her away.

"It isn't," she insisted, pulling back. "It's the dog's business. Who's going to save that dog?" She couldn't free herself from Brett's grasp, so she leered at the driver and, in a screech, threatened, "I'm going to report you, mister! You, you irresponsible jerk!" She kicked his tire. "The Humane Society is going to hear about this. I've got your license number."

The driver gunned his motor as the light up ahead switched to green. He pealed out, sending the dog skittering across the truckbed and crashing into the tailgate with a squeal.

"Oh, God." Chloe hid her eyes.

Brett ushered her back to the curb, weaving between oncoming traffic all the way. He leaned against a retaining wall at the corner and folded his arms. In silence he stood there, staring into space, his head resting against the cold granite blocks.

Chloe plunked her forehead against the stone. "I can't stand it," she said weakly.

"Yeah. Well, I can't either." Brett's voice brought Chloe's head up fast.

He faced her. "Don't ever do that again. You could have gotten yourself killed."

"I do it all the time," Chloe said. "Every time I see a dog riding in the back of a truck. It's so dangerous, Brett. Ignorant people need to be educated."

"What if he'd had a gun, Chloe? He could have blown your head off."

"Oh, come on—"

"Don't you watch TV? It happens all the time. Crazies shooting people from their cars for no apparent reason. Except in your case . . ." His voice trailed off. Closing his eyes, he turned away.

Chloe's indignation flared, but she allowed it to cool before responding, "If I don't do it, who will?"

"Someone else," he said. "Anyone. Just not you."

She opened her mouth to protest, but Brett wrapped his arms around her waist and pulled her close. He said softly, "I care about you, Chloe. I care a lot. I couldn't stand it if anything ever happened to you. Please, don't do it again. It scares me, okay?"

She swallowed hard. He was telling the truth, she realized from the thumping of his heart against hers. Okay, so maybe it was a little foolish. And risky. Maybe she could just step up her letter-writing campaign to the newspapers. She wondered if she wasn't fighting a losing battle anyway, trying to educate bucketheads.

"I just wish people were more responsible," she murmured into his chest. She inhaled deeply. Hooboy, he smelled so clean, so zesty.

"Bees," Dr. Mankewicz said, his eyes dancing. "Italian bees. The workers are bred to be gentle and the queens are the highest producers. They can lay up to two thousand eggs per day. I'll set up the hive out back under the apple tree."

Brett glanced across the table at Chloe. He looked like a freaked-out field mouse. She reassured him with a smile. "Dad," she turned to her father, who was swirling honey into his tea, "did you really order a beehive?"

"Super deluxe model." He smiled. "It comes with everything a new beekeeper needs: bee coveralls, veil, gauntlets, helmet, hive—and the bees, of course." He sipped his tea, wiggling his eyebrows at her over the rim.

Chloe sighed. "My father collects hobbies for a hobby," she explained to Brett.

His face registered complete confusion.

"Let's see," she counted on her fingers, "there was the worm farm in the basement, which was replaced a year ago by the transcontinental train set—thank heavens. The worms stunk. Then, there are the stamps and the coins and I don't know what-all crammed into his desk. The garage is wall-to-wall woodworking tools; they bit the sawdust years ago. And in the attic are the kites, oil paints, and tuba . . . did I forget anything, Dad?"

He mumbled something about "investments," and took another sip of tea.

Chloe said, "Oh, how could I forget the garden out back? Dad grows seafood."

She forked a green bean into her mouth. Both Brett and her father stared at her. She chewed and swallowed. "Crabgrass. Get it?"

Chloe's father chuckled. Brett gulped down his entire glass of iced tea in one swig. "Seconds on the sauerkraut?" Gran held out the still-heaping bowl of pickled cabbage toward Brett.

"No, thank you, Mrs. Mankewicz," he said, wiping his mouth with his twisted napkin. "I'm full. Everything was really good. Uh, great."

She set down the bowl, then rested her chin on her elbows and said, "Tell us, Hans. How are Blue October's plans proceeding for sabotaging the politburo?"

Chloe almost spit-sprayed the far wall. "Gran, why don't I help you clear these dishes?" She scootched back in her chair. Hauling her grandmother up by the elbows from behind, she signaled to her father to keep the conversation rolling.

"So, uh, Brett," he said, "Chloe tells me you dabble in football."

Chloe rolled her eyes. She grabbed Gran's plate

and Brett's, then nudged her grandmother into the kitchen. Behind her, she heard her father add, "I'm not too familiar with the game myself. I was a chess man in college. You've heard of the Orangutan opening, Mankewicz attack? I invented that."

Chloe moaned.

Later, after dinner, as Chloe accompanied Brett out to the driveway, he remarked, "Your family's, uh, interesting." He laced his fingers through hers. "Was your grandmother in the Holocaust or something?"

Chloe burst into laughter. "No, she's just OD'd on spy novels. You know, Ludlum and Clancy? Le Carré? She's an espionage junky. I like to think of it as her 'Bourne Identity crisis.' "

"Huh?" he said.

"She loves this one book, *The Bourne Identity*." Chloe shook her head. "Never mind." She didn't really want to tell him the truth, so she changed the subject. "What do you think of my father?"

Brett took Chloe's other hand. "It's hard to read him. You said he was an anthropology professor at the university, so I kind of expected . . . I don't know, this is stupid. Indiana Jones." He made a face at her. "I hope I did okay. He sort of intimidates me."

Chloe smiled. "He intimidates himself. Anyway, does it really matter what he thinks of you?" Chloe only wondered because she could read her father perfectly, and she knew that he was not bowled over by Brett.

"It matters, sure it matters," Brett said. "I don't want him to think some creep is taking out his daughter. I don't want him to worry about you, especially on those nights when I keep you out *real* late."

He was using that voice again. Chloe felt the tingle begin in the roots of her hair. "I, uh, better get back," she said, smooshing down her bun to keep it from lifting off. "Homework, you know." *Sure,* she added to herself, *as if you could concentrate on anything besides the scrumptiousness of those milk-chocolate eyes.*

He released her hands and began twisting a stray curl at Chloe's neck around his index finger. A movement drew their eyes to the picture window. Chloe's father stood there, conspicuously cleaning his glasses on the curtain sheers. Brett jerked his hand away. He started down the driveway, then turned and said, "I'll pick you up for school tomorrow. What time's your speech?"

"Oh, no, my speech." Chloe gasped. "I haven't even written it. Is it tomorrow? I'm not ready. I have to call Muriel. Good luck. I mean, good-bye. Good night." She screamed, "Good grief!" and raced for the house.

Chapter 9

Under a spray of moonbeams, Chloe lay stretched out across her window seat. She'd just begun to polish her speech when she heard a faint mewing. "Deaf?" she called, looking up. Deaf Leopard was in his usual spot on the bed, a camouflaged ball of fur against her giant stuffed panda. Chloe heard the sound again.

"What is that?" She set her notebook down and headed for the door. Outside on the landing the noise was louder, more distinct, like the whimpering of a wounded animal. A sound she recognized from the shelter.

She padded down the stairs, following the noise. It came from her grandmother's room at the end of the hall. Peering in through the cracked door, Chloe found Gran sitting on the edge of her bed, still fully clothed. The antique clock on her bureau chimed eleven.

"Gran?" Chloe pushed open the door.

Her grandmother gazed up at her with unseeing eyes. Eyes brimmed with tears.

"What is it, Gran? What's wrong?" Chloe sat next to her and took her hands.

"Chloe?" Her grandmother inhaled a shallow, quivery breath. "I can't remember . . ." She gazed at Chloe with panic-stricken eyes.

"What Gran? What can't you remember?" Chloe asked. She wiped a tear from her grandmother's cheek.

"My nightgown. Where is my nightgown?"

Chloe said, "Right here, Gran. Next to you." She reached around to pull the flannel gown into her grandmother's lap.

"I can't remember . . ." The gown untouched, she reached up to finger a button on her dress.

It took Chloe only a moment to realize what her grandmother had forgotten. "These little bitty buttons they sew on everything today are so irritating, aren't they? I swear, I can't work them through the holes myself." She removed her grandmother's dress and undergarments, then slipped the nightgown over her head. The whole time, her grandmother stared ahead into the darkness, mewling a little with each exhale of breath.

Chloe pulled back the covers and eased her grandmother into bed. She kissed her cheek and murmured, "I love you, Gran. Sleep well. And

65

don't worry, I'll be here in the morning to help you get dressed."

At the door, Chloe heard her grandmother whisper urgently, "Mishka, take the two-twenty to Lausanne. Bring nothing. Tell no one. We will have your papers when you arrive. Carry a rose, Mishka. A single red rose so that we will know you. Sub rosa. Remember, sub rosa."

Chloe blew her grandmother a kiss and pulled the door closed behind her.

Chloe feathered her hair around her shoulders, adjusted her beret, and stood up straight. Shoulders squared, she faced the mirror. "Remember, you have the right to refuse." She cleared her throat and started again. "You have an *obligation* to refuse. Put an end to senseless animal slaughter. There are so many alternative ways to study anatomy—computer simulations, robotics, in vitro cultures." Chloe moaned. "Too technical. You have to appeal to their emotions."

She set her shoulders again. "Consider, when you slice through the heart of a cat, that sweet, soft tabby may have been your little brother's or sister's. Think of children who cry themselves to sleep at night because their puppies are stolen. Yes, *stolen,* right out of their own backyards. Sold to high school biology classes and biomedical research labs. These people will stop at nothing to make a buck. The animals are subjected to painful experiments, psychological torture, diseases, surgery without anesthesia. And why? Because of *you*." She pointed. "You, who choose to dissect animals in class. You are condoning the slaughter of innocent rabbits and pigs and cats. . . ."

Chloe wrenched down her accusatory finger with her other hand. "Oh, God, *please* don't let me get carried away." She inhaled deeply to calm herself. *I wish Muriel were doing this,* she thought. *But if there's one fear she really does have, it's public speaking. She goes into shell shock whenever she gets on stage.* Chloe sighed. The doorbell rang, jolting her back to reality, and she hustled to gather her books.

At the bottom of the stairs, Chloe heard someone puttering around in the kitchen, so she took a quick detour. Gran stood at the stove. There was a wooden spoon in one of her hands, swirling a glop of smoking oatmeal, while the other hand propped open a dog-eared paperback on the counter. Earlier, Chloe had risen to make sure her grandmother was up and dressed.

Chloe turned off the burner under the oatmeal. "Big day, Gran." She kissed her on the cheek. "Gotta save some beasties from going under the knife."

Gran glanced up and nodded. "Yes, of course," she said. "The dagger must be buried with the corpse. Find the body and you'll find the murder weapon." She returned immediately to her novel.

Chloe smiled meekly. The bell sounded again, and she scampered. It was a crisp October day, the kind of morning that made the world smell fresh and free. Chloe filed it in her memory bank

67

under "E" for exhilarating. *Life is glorious,* she thought, smiling at Brett.

He took her books, then laughed. "Let's see your shirt."

She held open her jacket.

"That's great. 'Rats Have Rights, Too.' "

"I like it." Chloe beamed.

"I like you." He smiled and Chloe melted.

Her speech had its intended effect on the students at Aspen Grove Middle School. She knew it when she noticed row after row of sad faces. Only once did she stray from her index cards, when she got to the part about making a choice. As if there were any choice other than refusing to carve up animals. Muriel steered her back with a gesture from the front row to stay cool.

"Chloe, you were magnificent!" Muriel rushed up to her afterwards. "You really made people examine their consciences."

"Do you think so?" Chloe exhaled a long breath. "Thanks, Muriel. I was so nervous."

"You? I can't even imagine it. You were wonderful." She hugged her.

"Did you see Brett? What was his reaction?" Chloe peered over Muriel's shoulder to search the auditorium.

"Who knows?" Muriel shrugged. "You touched the people who care. The ones who really matter."

Chloe spotted him racing up the aisle toward the exit as fast as his muscled legs could carry him. "Brett!" she called, but he didn't acknowledge her before disappearing out the open double doors.

She was disappointed at first. By third period she was worried, and by lunchtime livid.

"Why didn't he come on stage and tell me I was good? I was good, wasn't I, Muriel? I mean, I didn't embarrass him or anything? Why would he leave without even saying 'way to go' or 'heck of a speech'? Whatever it is jocks say."

"You were fantastic," Muriel replied. "Forget about him. If it bothers him that you're outspoken about your beliefs, then he's just what we always suspected—a beef-for-brains."

"Don't, Muriel." Chloe turned on her friend. "I don't know what to think. I'm so angry—"

"Good speech, Chloe," a group of Brett's friends passed by congratulating her. She smiled half-heartedly, waving her thanks.

"I didn't think it was good," Brett's familiar voice rang in her ears.

Chloe's chin hit the table. "What did you say?"

He stood before her, impassive. Suddenly his face broke into a smile and he sauntered around behind the table. "I thought it was awesome."

Before Chloe could utter a word, Brett thrust a red rose at her. "Here, I got you this. It isn't much, but it's all the money I had." He leaned close to whisper in her ear. "Don't tell the coach where I went during PE. It took me like an hour to find a flower shop, then I had to sneak back in so I wouldn't get caught for ditching. I wanted to run up after your speech and kiss you right there." Then he kissed her, right there in the cafeteria with everyone watching.

"Have lunch with me," he said, his hands locked around her waist.

Even though Chloe was dazzled, she wasn't blinded to her responsibility. "I can't, Brett. The ARC table. I can't just leave."

"Muriel can handle it, can't you, Muriel?" He cocked his head over Chloe's shoulder at Muriel.

Muriel scowled.

"Come on. It's Chloe's big day. She should be among her fans. Her admiring fans, like me."

Chloe looked at Muriel, and felt her contempt. Chloe was torn. Behind the glower, she recognized in Muriel's eyes the plea to stay and share the glory with her. Then Brett pulled Chloe closer and smiled down on her.

That mesmerizing smile. Chloe turned to her friend. "Just for today, Mur. You can handle it, can't you? It's only an antivivisection pamphlet, and most people are just taking them on their way in. All you have to do is answer their questions." She whiffed at her rose, averting her eyes from Muriel's laser-like glare.

"No problem," Muriel said in a voice that splintered Chloe's spine. "It's *only* antivivisection. Go ahead. Your public awaits."

"Mur—"

"You're going to have to buy me lunch, Chloe," Brett said, pulling her away. "Unless you're willing to share this with me." He brushed the rose petals and smacked his lips.

Chloe pressed the flower to her chest. "Get back, Jack. Not even a starving vegetarian would eat her first rose."

Chapter 10

"You mean you don't even own a pair of jeans?" Brett bit off a hunk of veggie pizza and chewed. They were on their way to see *Dirty Double Cross* for the fourth time.

"I guess I never joined the jeans generation," Chloe said. "They're so, I don't know, conformist." She brightened. "But I do have a pair of overalls. With a red bandanna in the pocket and my *sombrero,* I could be Tex Mex."

Brett wrinkled his nose. "It's not that I don't like your clothes, Chloe. I mean, they're you and that's cool at school and stuff. But my parents are like ultimate yuppie conservos."

"What about my pin-striped CPA suit?" she said. "I have the whole getup—tailored pants, vest, suit coat. I think I even have a top hat."

"Chloe." Brett made a face at her. "This is

important to me." He handed her a slip of paper. "You can use my ten-dollars-off coupon for The Gap."

Not too subtle, Chloe thought. She sighed and gazed over his shoulder out the restaurant window. The blur of bustling shoppers made her dizzy. She swore she'd never shop at Westside Mall. Draper's Furs had an outlet there, and inside were two pet stores that sold live animals. The food court served all the worst products of factory farming: hamburgers, chicken, hot dogs, you name it.

Jeans. Chloe cringed at the thought. They were so . . . so ordinary.

She telephoned Muriel as soon as she got home. "I'd never ask a favor like this, Mur, but I'm a desperate person in a desperate situation."

"You sound desperate," Muriel said.

"I need you to come shopping with me at the mall for a pair of . . ." Chloe hissed through her teeth, "jeans."

There was silence on the other end. Finally, Muriel spoke. "In your own words: Are you lowering yourself to commit to conformity? Never mind, don't answer that. He's changing you."

"No, he's not." Chloe clucked. "Geez, Mur. It's just that he wants me to make a good impression on his parents. I'm going over there for dinner."

"What's wrong with the impression you already make?"

Chloe exhaled exasperatedly. "You have to

admit, the sight of me could create a major planetary disturbance in the yuppie cosmos."

"I don't know. *I* like your weirdness."

"Thanks." Chloe frowned. "I think. Anyway, will you go? I promise we won't even pass a cosmetics counter."

"Ignoring the problem won't make it go away. I quote you again."

"Muriel—"

"All right. But I'm wearing a disguise."

Half an hour later, Muriel showed up. She was sporting her little brother's Agent Orange-colored clown wig and a pair of Looney Tunes sunglasses. Chloe moaned, watching her weave down the street on her bike. Before she could change her mind, Chloe hopped on her bike and pedaled after Bozo.

"How do you like your steak, Chloe?" Brett's father slapped a sirloin on the Jenn-Air, while Chloe stifled a gag.

"On the cow," she answered, pleading salvation with her eyes at Brett.

He took Chloe's hand and led her out of the kitchen. Over his shoulder he said, "Just make it medium, Dad."

When they were in the hall, Chloe whispered, "Brett, why is your father making me a steak? Didn't you tell him?"

Brett shrugged. "If I'd told him you were a vegetarian, he wouldn't have bought the steak. And I wouldn't have gotten two." He smiled at her.

"Is that supposed to be funny?"

Brett sobered.

Chloe couldn't believe it. She already felt like the major freak at a sideshow with his perfectly preppie family gawking at her. Now dinner was going to be "serve Chloe up on a platter." If only Brett had let her wear the khakis with her flak jacket and helmet, she might've felt a little more protected.

When everyone sat down for dinner, Brett said, "I'll take that, Dad." He leaned over and stabbed the steak off the platter near Chloe's head. "Chloe doesn't eat meat."

The table grew so silent, Chloe could hear her own cells splitting. Or was that a headache?

"No meat at all?" Mrs. Ryan asked from the far end of the table.

Chloe shook her head. She felt the heat searing her cheeks.

"I knew about ham, but I didn't realize your people couldn't eat sirloin," she remarked.

Chloe frowned. "My people?"

"Herb Cohen eats steak," Mr. Ryan said, looking puzzled. "Just last week we had lunch at the The Ox Bow and he ordered a T-bone. He did complain about the quality of the beef afterwards, which always gripes me. Nothing's ever good enough for Herb."

Mrs. Ryan said to Chloe, with more than a hint of annoyance in her voice, "It's Grade A choice. I picked it out myself, eight dollars a pound."

Chloe understood then. She met Mrs. Ryan's

eyes. "I'm not Jewish," she said. "And I'm sure the steak is top grade. What self-respecting cow would have it any other way?"

Brett slapped her leg under the table. His father squawked, "Eight bucks a pound? For chrissakes, Doreen, who are we trying to impress here, the Queen of Sheba?"

Everyone looked at Chloe. *That'd be a stretch,* she thought, silently voicing their opinions. Swallowing hard, fighting to force back tears, Chloe mumbled, "Please pass the broccoli."

Chapter 11

"What do the two of you have in common, anyway?" Muriel asked.

"A lot," Chloe lied. Okay, she couldn't think of anything specific. But she knew by the bliss she felt whenever she and Brett were together that she was in love. "You know what they say: opposites attract."

Muriel finished resetting her watch to Greenwich time, which she did every Monday morning. "Is that what they mean by animal magnetism?"

Chloe narrowed her eyes. Muriel was starting to get on her nerves.

Muriel hurried off to class, leaving Chloe muttering to herself about informing Her Intellectual Mightiness, Muriel Blevins, that one cannot live on lust for married men alone, when Brett appeared at her locker. Tingling the back of her neck with his breath, he whispered, "I've missed you." Chloe dropped her Western Civ book on her foot.

He rested his forearm across the narrow rim of the locker door and fingered her fedora. "Tell your dad you'll be spending the night at Muriel's," he said.

Chloe looked up at him. "I don't want to lie to my father. I've never lied to him. Why does the party have to last all night?" She picked up her Civ book and shoved it onto the top shelf, then scanned the lower shelf for last week's *Time* and her current affairs folder.

Brett caught the two-ton Civ book as it slid off the shelf toward her head. "Like I said, Jensen's parents are out of town for the weekend, so he's having this all-night Halloween party." Jensen was Kenny's best friend in high school. Brett jiggled the book back into place, and added, "He's not inviting that many middle-school guys. Only the ones he respects; about ten of us from the football team. We should feel honored, Chloe. Plus, you won't believe the house he lives in. His dad's a pro golfer, you know."

"Pro putt-putt?"

Brett didn't answer. He didn't even smile.

Chloe bit her tongue. Her eyes fell. "I'm not going to lie to my father. We'll just have to be back by ten."

"Oh, Chloe." He rapped on the neighboring locker a few times with his fist.

Chloe felt his disappointment, in tremors, as

78

he stared off down the hall over her head. She slammed her locker door closed and ducked under his arm. Then, gazing up at him, she added, "Maybe I could persuade Dad to let me stay out until eleven."

His face brightened, but only a glimmer before dimming again. "I was really looking forward to our first all-nighter."

Our first what? Chloe's stomach lurched. *Hooboy,* she thought. *Maybe I can persuade Dad to order me home before dark.*

The party was a mob scene. "Jensen respects more people than I even know," Chloe thought out loud. She squeezed Brett's hand for reassurance. "You look scary," she yelled to him over the din.

"Rrrrrroar," he growled back. They'd decided to dress as endangered species. Even though she was secretly dying to go as Rhett and Scarlett, she couldn't get up the nerve to suggest it. Brett was a Rwandan mountain gorilla, and she was a Pacific green turtle—at least that's what they were supposed to be. The closest thing they could find at Clothes Encounters, the costume rental store, was King Kong and a Ninja turtle. Chloe absolutely refused to wear the Donatello rubber mask, though. Instead, she topped off the turtle shell with her green pillbox.

She'd scoffed at Muriel's suggestion to go as an animal rights activist. Muriel was just mad because Chloe had asked her if she'd mind manning the ARC table two days a week, so Chloe could eat lunch with Brett. Twice a week, was it so much to ask?

Turk appeared out of a wrinkle in the crowd with his new girlfriend, Jackye, with a y, Chloe presumed. They were dressed as two peas in a pod. "Hey, what are you guys supposed to be?" Turk said. "The tortoise and the hairy?" He cracked himself up. Jackye giggled.

"Make like a pea and split," Chloe muttered.

Turk curled a lip at her.

"Where's the food, pea brain?" Brett asked through his breathing hole between the fangs. Turk pointed. He and Turk exchanged insults for a while, which gave Chloe a chance to survey the party crowd. There were some pretty wild costumes, upside-down men and belly dancers, Draculas and Madonna look-alikes. Over in the corner, a few couples were making out.

Brett removed his gorilla head, leaned down, and kissed Chloe. "You want to—"

"No," she said.

He gave her a funny look. "Vegetarians don't dance?"

"Dance? Oh, uh, sure. I love to dance."

He wrapped a hairy paw around her shoulders and ushered her out onto the patio dance floor. Thirty minutes later, after rocking out inside a sweltering rubber turtle shell, crushed by a thousand other hot bodies, Chloe felt faint. "Could we get something to drink?" She fanned her face.

They found the ice chest in the kitchen and

80

dug out a couple of Cokes. Turk and Jackye joined them. For a joke, Turk shook Jackye's can before handing it to her, and when she popped the top, it exploded in foam. She lurched backward, right into Chloe, who fell against a couple of high school guys.

"Hey, watch it," one of them snarled, but not before his drink sloshed all over Chloe's costume.

"Oh, great," she mumbled. Now she wouldn't get her deposit back. She sniffed the shell and snarled back at the guy, "You know, it's illegal to drink at your age."

He sneered. "You gonna call the cops?"

Brett yanked her away. "Sorry," he called over her shoulder. "No problem."

"Why are you apologizing to them?" Chloe said. She reeked of beer. "If the cops show up, we're all going to get arrested."

"That's Jensen," Brett whispered.

"Yeah, so? Do his parents know he's drinking?"

Brett just looked at her. "He called and got permission, okay? Come on, Chloe, lighten up. We're here to have fun. Nobody's drinking." He held her eyes.

She broke the staredown and glanced around. Now she wondered what all the plastic cups were full of. Maybe she didn't want to know.

Chloe had to admit, she was having fun. Brett knew everyone, and when they talked to him, they included her. Every once in a while, Brett would lean down and kiss her. She felt good, special. Like being Brett's girlfriend was an honor.

They danced and ate and drank. As the night air cooled, the party moved inside. Chloe didn't even realize that they'd all crushed into the basement when she heard someone's wristwatch alarm beep and beep and beep.

"Brett," she said, "What time is it?"

He checked his watch. "Uh-oh." He showed her. Chloe freaked.

It took forever to find Kenny and drag him away, so by the time Chloe got home, it was after midnight. When she opened the door to tiptoe in, the foyer flooded with light. There, looming in silhouette at the end of the hall, was her father.

Chapter 12

Dr. Mankewicz perched stiffly across from Chloe at the dining-room table, hands folded in front of him. "I want you to break it off," he said.

"Can't we talk about this in the morning, Dad? I mean, later in the morning. Like in the afternoon? Say, tomorrow or next week?" Chloe yawned.

His eyes bore into the wall behind her head. "I don't think you understand the seriousness of this situation. Number one, you've been drinking."

"I have not!"

"You smell like beer."

"Oh, that. Someone spilled a drink on me. But we weren't drinking."

"Who was? The person who drove you home?"

"No." *I don't think so,* Chloe added to herself.

Had Kenny been drinking? She'd never thought to ask, just jumped in the car to rush home.

"Number two," her father went on. "You violated your curfew."

"I didn't mean to. We lost track of time."

"Number three, you are not the same person you were before you met this boy. I want that other Chloe back, the one I could trust."

She focused on her father's face. His very intense face. "You can trust me. You can trust Brett, too. Come on, Dad. I said I was sorry."

"Sorry doesn't cut it."

Chloe exhaled exasperatedly. "What do you want me to do? Tell Brett to take a hike?"

"The farther the better."

Chloe's jaw dropped. "You're serious."

"Damn right."

"Dad!" she gasped. She'd never heard him swear in all her life. "You can't mean it." She swallowed the sickness rising in her throat. "No." She shook her head. She rose slowly from her chair. "I can't. I won't. I . . . love him."

A heavy stillness descended on the room. Chloe felt the weight on her shoulders. "You can't keep us apart," she said. "What are you going to do, confine me to my room? Hire a bodyguard?"

He looked up and locked eyes with her. "No. I'm simply going to ask you to obey me. Stop seeing him."

Hot tears welled in her eyes. "Don't do this, Dad. Please," she pleaded.

He turned and looked away.

The tears flooded down her face. Whirling, Chloe fled from the room. She raced up the stairs, slammed her door, and fell on her bed, sobbing. Deaf burrowed in under her shoulder, purring. "Leave me alone," she said and pushed him away.

A locomotive roared through Chloe's head. She jerked awake. Glancing at her digital clock, which read seven-fifteen, she prayed, "Oh, please, God. Make last night just a bad dream."

A whistle shrieked and Chloe groaned. She pulled the panda over her head. The noise continued—the chugging of an engine, followed by the whoo-whoo of a whistle.

Chloe staggered to her feet and slipped into her robe. Sometime during the night, or early morning, she must've gotten up to take off her costume. It lay on the floor by her closet, a smelly lump of rubber.

At the bottom of the stairs, Chloe saw that the basement door was open a crack, so she shuffled toward it. She had a pounding headache. All the way down the rickety wooden steps, she clung to the railing for dear life. On the last step, Chloe pulled her bathrobe cord tight around her waist, folded her arms, and rested her throbbing head against the cement wall. "You've resurrected the Orient Express," she said to him.

Her father didn't look up. Instead, he pulled a lever at the far end of the tracks that switched the oncoming train to an alternate route, through a tunnel marked "To Europe." Whooooooo-whoooooo. He leaned on the whistle.

Chloe winced. "Can we talk?"

Without so much as a glance in her direction, he said, "Go ahead."

"About last night." She watched the train take a wide arc at Brussels, then pick up speed as it headed toward Amsterdam. "I apologize," she said. "I promise I'll never come home late again."

He pressed a button that sent a cough of smoke up the engine's smokestack. Whoooooo-whoooooo.

"Quit that, Dad. It hurts." Chloe pressed her palms to her temples. She swallowed hard. "About Brett . . ." The express came zooming toward her. Whoooooooooo-whoooooooooo. "Dad, will you shut that damn thing off?"

He glanced up at her then. Shifting his attention back to the speeding bullet, he said, "There's nothing to talk about."

The train raced by Chloe, across Finland, speeding toward Russia. Right in front of her, it derailed. Her father grumbled, "Would you put the Pullman back on track?"

She shot him an icy glare. Without a word, she stomped up the stairs. At the top, Gran leaped out from the kitchen, wielding a celery stalk. "Traitor," she snarled at Chloe. "Defector," she accused.

"You're crazy," Chloe muttered, and brushed by her.

She stood in the shower until it ran cold. Shivering, she dried herself, took two aspirin, and went back to bed. But she couldn't sleep. She couldn't win the war that raged in her head.

How could she stop seeing Brett? What she'd told her father was true. She loved him. She couldn't bear the thought of not seeing him anymore. But she loved her father too, and she'd never defy him.

The phone rang downstairs. When no one picked it up, it stopped. A minute later it rang again, and again. Fifteen minutes later the doorbell dinged, and dinged, and dinged. Chloe hollered, "Can't a person even rot in peace around here?" She flung back the covers and threw on her robe. When she heaved open the front door, Muriel blew in out of a blizzard.

"Where have you been?" she asked, stamping off the sticky clumps of snow from her boots. "I have fantastic news. Also, Angela Herrera's been trying to get hold of you to find out if you're planning to go to the shelter today. She says you were scheduled to work this morning. Whew," Muriel unzipped her coat, "it's really coming down out there."

"What time is it?" Chloe mumbled. She took Muriel's wet coat and tossed it into the hall closet. "When did it start to snow?" Maybe she'd taken a longer shower than she'd thought. "What month is this?"

Before Muriel could speak, Chloe's father appeared from out of the basement. When their eyes met down the long hallway, Chloe glared daggers at him. She turned her back and tromped up the stairs ahead of Muriel.

Muriel said behind her, "It's one o'clock. November first. Aren't you even up yet? Wait till you hear the incredible news."

"I'm sick," Chloe said, crawling back into bed.

"Oh, Chloe, I'm sorry." Muriel plopped down on the bed beside her. "How thoughtless of me to just barge in here. Did you catch that flu virus that's going around? My brother got it; it's horrid. He's barfing all over everything. Do you have a fever?" She felt Chloe's forehead.

"If I don't, I'm going to work one up," Chloe muttered. "Do me a favor, Mur. Call Angela and tell her I can't make it today."

"Sure. But that wasn't the only reason she was trying to get hold of you. She wanted to tell you herself, but you know me." Muriel shrugged. "For some reason I cannot keep a secret. Maybe I have concealaphobia." She giggled at her joke.

"Get on with it, Mur," Chloe said. "I have a date with death."

Muriel bounced on the edge of the bed, jerking Chloe's neck around like a tetherball. Her headache roared back. Chloe snuggled up against Deaf and squeezed her eyes shut to concentrate on Muriel's words.

". . . a bill being introduced to the legislature that would require all animal research in the state to be justified scientifically. Not only that, there'd be a ban on the sale of cosmetics and household products not labeled 'cruelty-free.' This is so incredible, Chloe. If we can get it passed, it'll be the first step in totally eliminating all testing on animals. It'd be a model for the whole nation."

Chloe shared Muriel's enthusiasm, even though all she could work up was a weak, "Wow."

"There's more. Listen," Muriel went on. "The ASPCA is going to be here, the National Antivivisection Society and—get this—PETA! It's finally happening, Chloe. What we've always dreamed of. The end of animal slaughter!"

Chloe smiled, then squinched at the ensuing pain. "It is exciting, Mur. Really exciting. But can we talk about it tomorrow? I need to sleep—"

"You haven't even heard the exciting part!"

Chloe stifled a groan as Muriel bounced again.

"At the committee hearing, the Humane Society wants to include the voice of youth, so to speak. Angela suggested you. The vote was unanimous. They want Chloe Mankewicz to be their keynote speaker."

It took Chloe's numb ears a minute to absorb what Muriel had said. She opened her eyes and they widened. "Me?"

Nodding, Muriel bit her lip. "Isn't it thrilling? To be a pioneer, a leader in the movement? Oh, Chloe. Haven't you just prayed for this day? We've worked so long and hard, you especially. Your convictions have always carried me, you know that. And now you have a chance to influence thousands, maybe millions." She squeezed

Chloe's hand through the covers. "I'm so proud to be your friend."

Chloe gulped as she watched Muriel's eyes fill with tears. Could she do this? Be the voice of youth? At a state legislative hearing? Well, of course she could do it. She'd given dozens of speeches before. With all her heart she believed in the movement. So why did she feel hesitant? Reluctant? The fact that this law, if passed, would destroy her mother's career couldn't possibly have anything to do with it, could it?

Chloe flipped open her mental journal to start a new list: *People who already hate me or who are going to hate me,* she scribbled in think ink, *depending on the decisions I am about to make:*

1. *My father*
2. *My mother*
3. *My best friend*
4. *My boyfriend . . .*

She paused. Deaf purred and rubbed against her cheek. *No, you don't make the list, sweetie,* she sent him a mental message. *No matter what I did, you'd always love me. That's the thing about animals. They don't have the capacity to hate. There is someone else, though.*

She refilled her mind's inkwell. Then she added the last entry:

5. *Myself*

Chapter 13

It was a devastating decision, but what choice did she have? What could she do, go live with her mother? It wasn't even an option.

"I can't see you anymore," she told Brett on the phone. She'd never called a boy before. She even got him out of bed.

"Because of last night?"

Chloe blinked back tears.

Brett said, "We didn't even do anything. Did you tell him that?"

"He doesn't care. He forbids me to see you."

Brett let out a short breath. "Parents. I hate them. Chloe—"

"I'm sorry, Brett. Good-bye." She slammed down the phone and raced upstairs, tears streaming down her cheeks.

* * *

The breakup left a gaping hole in Chloe's heart. A place once filled with unconditional love for her father. She couldn't bear to be in the same room with him, refused to speak to him, didn't acknowledge his existence. It hurt him, she knew it, but she wanted her father to feel her pain. Deep and hard.

It wasn't so easy to avoid Brett. He kept hanging around. He was always there—by her locker, in the halls, in the cafeteria. He invaded her space, her thoughts. He wouldn't let her go.

"We could see each other in secret," he'd suggested.

She'd thought about it, thought about it seriously. And decided she couldn't live that way, sneaking around behind her father's back. "No," she told Brett. "I'm sorry. I can't."

It was the bouquet of roses that finally sent Chloe over the edge. They were delivered to her house Friday after school. The card read, "Rats have rights, too. Come back, Chloe. I love you. B."

After that, she couldn't even motivate herself to get out of bed in the morning. For a week she just lay there, feigning flu, and staring at the roses as they shriveled. She shriveled with them. *Chloe the comatose.* She liked the sound of that. *Chloe the vegetable.* She liked that even better. She buried her face in Deaf Leopard and slept.

Muriel stopped by every day after school; and as much as Chloe wanted to, needed to, talk to someone, she knew Muriel wasn't the one. She was afraid her best friend would side with her father.

Instead, they worked on the speech for the legislative committee hearing. Or rather, Muriel worked on the speech while Chloe stared blindly out the bay window, unconsciously stroking Deaf Leopard and herself into a stupor.

"Listen to this study, Chloe. You might want to include it. Researchers at the University of Oregon amputated the forelimbs of white mice to determine its effect on grooming behavior. Conclusion: The animals still tried to groom themselves with their limb stubs. Isn't that gruesome?"

Chloe sighed.

On Saturday she dragged herself out of bed and down to the Aspen Grove Animal Shelter. She hoped that a little unselfish giving might boost her sagging spirits. It didn't. Late in the afternoon, a sweet Beagle puppy was brought in. It'd been thrown from a truck bed into highway traffic and was so severely injured that it had to be put down. The puppy's cries of agony echoed in Chloe's ears all the way home.

Chloe found her father in the dining room nursing a cup of tea. "Hi," he called, looking up expectantly. "Where've you been? I called the shelter. . . ."

Chloe turned away. By now the ice floe between them had frozen over solid. "Chloe, I should warn you—"

She tuned him out. She didn't figure her life

could get any worse. It wasn't until she dragged into her bedroom and closed the door behind her that she discovered it could.

"What are you doing in my stuff?" Chloe threw her bag on the bed and stormed across the room. She grabbed her Rhett Butler doll out of her mother's grasp.

"I was admiring your collection. You never told me you were into *Gone With The Wind.*"

"I'm not *into* anything," Chloe snarled.

They had a brief staredown before Chloe whirled and resettled her RB doll on the shelf next to Scarlett.

"Is that your boyfriend, the picture you taped to Rhett's face?" her mother asked.

Chloe felt the blood rush to her cheeks. *Whatever possessed me to do that?* she asked herself, ripping the tiny yearbook picture off and crumpling it.

"He's cute," she said. "He reminds me of a boyfriend I once had in college. I don't remember his name, there were so many. We must share a preference for blondes." She smiled at Chloe.

Oh, brother, Chloe groaned inwardly. She kicked off her wet rubber boots and crawled into the window seat. Curling into a tight ball, she ground her chin into her knees. Her mother encroached on her space, examining the posters of endangered species, leafing through her closet, petting her cat. When Deaf weaved through her mother's legs, Chloe mouthed to him, "Traitor."

"You probably wondered why I chose your father to marry," her mother said. With a girlish giggle, she shook her head. "That mop of bushy hair, and believe me back then he had twice as much as he does now, *plus* a beard. It's too bad you inherited that from him—not the beard." She smiled at Chloe.

Chloe curled a lip.

"Fortunately," her mother continued, "you got my nose and skin."

"Mother, is there a point to this?"

She picked up Chloe's November issue of *Vegetarian Times,* the one with the tofu turkey on the cover, and set it back down on the bed. "He was an activist too, your father. Always involved in some cause—nuclear war, Vietnam, the starving children of Africa. He didn't have the time of day for someone like me. A college cheerleader—horrors!" The corners of her mother's tangerine lips turned up. "But I somehow managed to reel him in."

She reached into Chloe's cedar chest and fished out the fedora, which she placed on her head in front of the full-length mirror. "Physical beauty, that's what attracts men. I don't mean to say character isn't important. It is. But like most southern belles, I was brought up to believe that a woman who nurtures her outer beauty will naturally blossom within."

Chloe groaned audibly.

Her mother pursed her lips. She removed the

fedora and reached for the hat on the bureau. Chloe's green pillbox.

Like a bullet Chloe shot across the room. She rescued the hat from her mother's clutches. "Don't," Chloe said. "That one's . . ." *sacred,* she didn't say. "What are you doing here anyway, Mother?" She set the pillbox back on the bureau.

Her mother lowered herself onto Chloe's bed and patted the spot next to her. "Let's talk."

Resigning herself to the inevitable, Chloe perched rigidly beside her mother. Was she going to mention the cruelty-free committee? Chloe wondered. Would there be an argument, another verbal skirmish over misplaced loyalties? She braced for the assault.

"Your father called me. He wanted to talk about sex."

That's a relief, Chloe thought. Her head shot up. "What did you say?" Her eyes widened at her mother's reflection in the mirror.

Her mother laughed. "I thought that might get your attention. Actually, he wanted some advice about, how shall I put this delicately? He says you're boy-crazy."

"What!" She turned to face her. "For your information, *and* his, I am *not* boy crazy. I'm just crazy about one boy." *Oh, brother, why did I say that?* she chided herself.

Her mother smiled. "Of course you are." She extended a hand to stroke Chloe's flaming cheek, but Chloe recoiled. "Your father's overreacting, as usual. And I told him so."

Chloe's eyebrows arched. "You did?"

She nodded. "He told me what happened the night of the Halloween party, along with his totally inept handling of the situation." She shook her head. "I shouldn't be so hard on him. He does love you. If he could, he'd have you banished to some faraway kingdom. His little princess Chloe."

"Oh really, Mother." Chloe rose to her feet and leaned against the bureau, arms folded.

"It's the truth, darling. Fatherly love. No boy is ever good enough for daddy's little darling. Eccentric as your father is, he's no exception there."

Chloe thought she'd have to mull that over for a while. Accepting that her mother could confer even a quark of wisdom would take a cosmic event of some significance.

"I told him he made a mistake by forbidding you to see—what's his name?"

"Brett," Chloe mumbled. Her eyes strayed to the floorboard under her mother's stiletto heels.

"Brett. Rhymes with Rhett, doesn't it?"

Chloe met her mother's teasing eyes. She seethed.

Her mother rose and smoothed her fitted skirt over her thighs. "After some discussion, he agreed," she said. "Even though he is a stubborn old coot, like his mother. Who, by the way, should be committed. Do you know she snuck up behind me today, jabbed a carrot in my back, and demanded I surrender the computer chip?"

Chloe sucked in a smile.

"I told your father how unfair it was to expect a girl your age to take care of a dotty old woman. I don't suppose he pays you to be her caregiver?"

"Mother!" Chloe was aghast at the suggestion.

"I didn't think so. Getting back to the original discussion, your father does see the logic in allowing you to grow up, since he can't seem to stop the process. Unfortunately, none of us can." She sighed. Leaning into the mirror, she stretched her eyes taut at the temples.

Chloe glanced up into her mother's reflection. *She really is beautiful,* Chloe thought. *For someone her age. Should I tell her? No. I wouldn't want her to build any more character from within. Anyway, I'm still trying to figure out what she just said. Did she mean . . . ?*

"You'd better go call him, darling," her mother answered Chloe's unspoken question. Pivoting in place, she headed off across the room, heels clicking like a metronome on the hardwood floor. She paused at the door to wriggle her fingers into leather gloves before adding, "We wouldn't want him to find somebody else while you're pining away up here in Tara."

Chloe sneered at her mother's back as she exited. "By the way, dear," she poked her head in again, "I received a call from the Marketing Director last week down in Dallas." Chloe detected the slightest hint of a southern accent. "She told me there was a bill coming up in the legislature that would literally outlaw Desiree Cosmetics in this state. It has something to do with animal rights. Are you by any chance involved?"

Chloe swallowed hard. Then she squared her shoulders and said, "Of course I'm involved. Why wouldn't I be?"

Her mother pursed her lips. "Well, I'm late for my makeover," she said and slammed the door behind her.

Chapter 14

No sooner had the lavender Lexus backed down the driveway than Chloe was out the bedroom door and down the stairs. Grabbing a jacket, she smiled at her father, hopefully reassuring him that he was doing the right thing. He shrugged, but she saw the relief flood his face.

Chloe knew Brett would be at the football field. It was Saturday. Saturday meant football. Racing across the school's front lawn, she heard the final whistle along with the echo of cheers from the bleachers. By the time she reached the field, all the players were in the locker room.

"Rats," Chloe muttered. She smiled to herself, remembering. Rats have rights, too. She retreated to the front hallway and chewed on her knuckles, waiting.

A few minutes later, players began to emerge

from the gym, hauling duffel bags. As they met with their friends and families, Chloe stood on her tiptoes, straining to catch sight of Brett.

Finally, she spotted him sauntering down the hall next to Turk. Questions flashed through her mind: *What if my mother was right? What if he's given up on me? What if he's meeting somebody else? Somebody new.*

Brett stopped to talk to one of the cheerleaders. Chloe felt a shiver of fear slither down her spine. A minute later, Brett left Turk with the cheerleader and headed Chloe's way.

She watched anxiously as he jockeyed his duffel over his shoulder and trundled toward her, head down. *I don't know whether I'm going to burst into laughter or tears,* she thought. She nearly bit through her knuckle.

He glanced up suddenly and saw her. His pace slowed almost to a stop, then he began to trot. The trot turned into a sprint. In front of the trophy case, he dropped his duffel and grabbed her shoulders.

She smiled up at him. "I'm baa-aack."

Chloe's life returned to normal, as normal as it could be, considering. There were changes; love always brings change. Now they were officially a couple. Brett and Chloe. Chloe and Brett. They ate lunch together three, sometimes four times a week, while Muriel held down the ARC table. They had a standing date after school, either at Cal's Tex Mex or Brett's house. Muriel said she didn't mind walking home alone, although Chloe felt a little pang of guilt every time she left her standing at the door.

Football was Brett's consuming passion. Chloe didn't exactly share his fervor, but she did try. The Aspen Grove Cougars were winning, going to the play-offs, and she couldn't help getting swept up in the spirit of victory. So what if she was sandwiched between the spirit squad and the band at the games? So what if she was beginning to recite the school cheers in her sleep? So what if Brett asked her to wear jeans to the games instead of her East Indian wraparound? Maybe love means never having to see your sari.

To spend more time with Brett, Chloe cut back on her hours at the animal shelter, too. Only temporarily, she told herself, until football season was over.

"A love slave, that's what she called me," Chloe told Brett as he walked her to the animal shelter on Sunday afternoon. She clucked, remembering her latest exchange with Muriel.

"A love slave?" Brett smiled down on Chloe. "I think I like the sound of that."

The snow crunched under their feet. "I don't understand her," Chloe continued. "I'm just as committed as I've always been to the movement. Okay, so she didn't want to work the ARC table by herself. Why does that make it my fault that the whole thing was abandoned? I'm still the voice of youth at the legislative committee hearing, even though *she's* writing the whole speech." Chloe huffed. "Oh, that doesn't bother me, but she accused you of possessing me. She said you're making me compromise my principles. I don't see you choking any cheeseburgers down me." She looked up at him. "Do you think I'm an arm ornament?"

"A what?"

"You know. Someone with no identity. A decoration. An extension of somebody else."

He laughed. "That's definitely not you, Chloe. I think of you more as . . . a hood ornament."

She slugged him in the arm. "Maybe I should change my name to Chloy, with a Y, just to fit in. And while we're on the subject of principles, have you been thinking about what I asked you? You know, becoming a vegetarian?" She arched an eyebrow at him.

He sighed. "Let's not get into that again."

"Do you enjoy eating animal corpses?"

He made a face at her. "That's gross."

"It is gross. That's the whole point. Think about the dead flesh and chemicals you're putting into your body."

"I didn't think you had any complaints about my body."

Chloe blushed. "You know what I mean."

He took her mittened hand. She felt her conviction waning fast. "Think about the animals, Brett," she said quickly. "Six billion are slaughtered every year for food, and that's just in the U.S. Did you know that if everyone became a vegetarian we'd have four tons of grain for every starving person in the world?"

He released her hand. "Do you and Muriel sit around and memorize the encyclopedia, or what? Look, Chloe. I respect your beliefs, I really do. But don't force them on me, okay? Besides, I can't give up meat. I'm an athlete. We need meat for protein."

"No, you don't," Chloe's voice regained confidence as she scooted around to face him. "You can get all the protein you need from peanut butter, broccoli, soybeans, lentils. In fact, there's more protein in seaweed than there is in beef."

He smacked his lips. "Oh, yum. Pass the algae."

She smiled smugly. She had an argument he couldn't refute. "I've been doing some research, Brett. Did you know Bill Walton is a vegetarian?"

He widened his eyes at her. "The ex-basketball player?"

"I guess. And Murray Rose, an Australian, won three Olympic gold medals in swimming when he was only seventeen. He was a vegetarian. And Bill Pearl, he's a four-time Mr. Universe weight-lifter—"

Brett held up his hand. "Enough, Chloe. Don't push me. I'll think about it, okay?" He shook his head. Then he smiled, reached up, and yanked her beret down over her face. He took off, and she chased him all the way to the shelter.

"I'll pick you up at five," Brett said, leaning over to kiss Chloe. "Want to go out tonight? Turk's back with Alyssya, and he thought we might all go for pizza. You know, for old times' sake."

"Gee, sorry," Chloe said. "I have homework." *From last month,* she added to herself. "Plus, I promised Muriel—"

"That you'd read your *National Geographics* together?" He wrinkled his nose.

Brett was shielding his shoulder from Chloe's fist when the door to the shelter flew open and Angela Herrera came charging out. "Chloe, I'm so glad you're here," she said, out of breath. "There's no one else working today, and I need you at the desk. I just got an emergency call."

"What is it, Angela?" Chloe asked. She hoisted her bag over her shoulder.

"It's those religious fanatics who took over the church up past the mall. We just got an anonymous phone tip that they're planning to sacrifice a lamb at their service today."

"Oh, no!" Chloe's stomach lurched. "You can't go up there alone, Angela. I'm coming with you."

"No, you're not," Brett said, gripping her arm. "The weirdos in those religious cults are totally whacked out. If you interfere, there's no telling what they'll do."

Chloe tried to wrench away, but he held firm. "Brett, they're going to kill a lamb. A little lamb, for heaven's sake!"

He looked from Chloe to Angela and back to Chloe. "I'm coming with you," he said.

Angela turned the closed sign over and locked the door. "Come on, then. My truck's around back."

Chapter 15

A dozen cars filled the first rows of the church parking lot. Angela swerved her truck into an empty space and killed the engine.

"So, what do we do now?" Brett asked. "Put the sheets on?"

Chloe clucked. She got out of the truck and stood on the plowed blacktop, inspecting the grounds and listening. *It seems quiet enough,* she thought. *Too quiet. There should be an organ playing or voices. Singing, praying, some sign of religious fervor.* She headed toward the church.

Brett and Angela flanked her. "What are we going to do?" Angela whispered, hooking her arm in Chloe's.

"We're going to church," Chloe said. "It's Sunday, isn't it?"

"You're nuts," Brett muttered.

"Nuts are full of protein, too." She smiled up at him.

He shook his head.

At the entrance, Chloe yanked on the carved wooden handle of one of the big double doors. It opened. Dark. Eerie. She stepped inside, trailed closely by Angela and Brett. She could feel their shallow breathing on the back of her neck as her eyes adjusted to the shadowy vestibule.

"Okay. There's no one here," Brett said. "Let's go."

Chloe turned to him. "Don't you think that's strange, with all the cars in the parking lot?" She made a face at him. Then she marched across the vestibule and up the center aisle with Brett whispering urgently behind her, "Chloe, come back here."

At the altar she touched her green beret and thought, *Befitting attire, Chloe. Maybe I should have packed an apple grenade. This is so bizarre. Where is everyone?*

"Chloe, come here. Listen." Angela motioned Chloe over near the flickering votive candles, where she stood with her ear to the door.

Chloe followed the altar railing. She cupped her ear next to Angela's. "Voices," she said. "There must be a basement." She reached for the doorknob. "Let's go."

"Just a minute." Brett's hand covered hers. "This is insane. I'll go first."

Chloe beamed up at him. "My hero."

Turning the knob and pulling open the door,

he muttered, "We're going to die. You know that, don't you?"

She sucked in a smile.

There was a landing halfway to the basement where the three of them crouched to survey the goings-on. Chloe counted four people dressed in drab robes. They were circling a makeshift altar in the center of the room, intoning incantations. The rest of the congregation was filled in around them on folding metal chairs, heads bowed.

Chloe heard something else. A faint sound, yet distinct and familiar. Whimpering? No, more like whining. Was it the baa of a lamb? She squinted through the dusky basement light.

There in the corner sat a metal cage, and inside a white animal covered with curly fur. Chloe elbowed Angela, then Brett, and pointed. Angela gasped. Under his breath Brett said, "Geeeezus."

One of the robed men walked to the back and picked up the cage. At the next sound, Chloe and Angela both pricked up their ears. In unison they announced to each other, "It's a dog."

"A miniature poodle," Chloe added, straining to get a better look. "Is lamb out of season, or what?"

"Don't joke around, Chloe," Brett said. "This is serious."

Angela grabbed her arm. "Look, he has a knife. I think he's actually going to kill that poodle."

"Not if I can help it." Chloe stood erect. She charged for the stairs, jerking away from Brett's lunge for her arm. "Excuse me here, but are you people for real?" she asked.

A clamorous scooting of chairs echoed in the basement. People murmured in low voices, some falling to their knees. Chloe announced, "We're from the Aspen Grove Animal Shelter. We received a report that you were planning to sacrifice a live animal here today. Is that true?" She'd reached the altar and was addressing one of the men in the robes, the one with the knife.

He glowered at her. "What right do you have to barge in here? This is a sacred ceremony."

"Sacred?" Chloe scoffed. "More like illegal. I'm sure the police will want to hear all about it. Come here, sweetheart," she cooed to the poodle, sticking a finger in through the wire to calm the dog. At the same time, she reached for the cage handle.

A cold hand plunged over hers. "Do you have a search warrant?"

She stared up into the hooded black eyes. "Officer Ryan, show him the search warrant," she called over her shoulder.

Brett stopped dead at the bottom of the stairs. He locked eyes with Chloe. A silent message passed from his head to hers: *We're going to die.*

What happened next was just like Hollywood, Chloe imagined. The vice squad burst through the door, saving the day. They weren't vice, exactly; just animal-control officers. Angela had had the presence of mind to call the sheriff's department before she'd left.

After giving a statement to the officers, Brett, Angela, and Chloe left with the poodle. By the time they got back to the shelter, it was closing time.

On the way to her house, Chloe replayed the afternoon's events out loud. Her giggling grew to hysterics. She didn't notice Brett turning off into Grisham Park until he'd stopped dead in his tracks behind her. "Let's take a detour," he said.

Holding hands, they started down the shoveled path. They passed the snow-heaped swings to the statue of Buffalo Bill in the center of the promenade.

"Did you know Buffalo Bill got his name because he could slaughter buffalo faster than anyone else?" Chloe shook her head. "Unbelievable, isn't it, that he's such a folk hero—"

"Chloe, I want you to quit," he cut her off. He sat on the toe of Buffalo Bill's boot and pulled her close to him.

"Talking about it so much, you mean? I know I get carried away with the movement."

"Not talking," he answered. "Not believing. Doing. I want you to quit the shelter. It's too dangerous. After today . . ." He exhaled a stream of breath.

Chloe threw her arms around his neck and gave a short laugh. "Come on, Officer Ryan. It's not always that exciting. We haven't had a sacrificial poodle in, I don't know how long. Although, we did get a firebomb threat last week after we rescued an injured pit bull from this jerk's garage."

"See?" He held her back. "The stuff you're involved in, this animal rights activism, it scares me. You're invading people's privacy. One day someone's going to come back at you. You're going to get hurt, Chloe. You, personally."

She shrugged. "Hey, at least I'll know I'm making an impression."

"Are you trying to be a martyr?" His voice took on a sharp edge.

She sobered. "Not intentionally. But if that's what it takes . . ."

He stood up and turned his back to her. "I don't understand you. I don't see how saving a bunch of dumb animals is something to risk your life over."

Chloe was stunned. Offended. How could he mean that? Didn't he know her at all? Didn't he understand about the movement? How it affected everything she did, everything she was? Was he one of *them* after all? She tried to banish the thought, but it lingered. It left a bad taste in her mouth. She thought she knew him, but this . . . now *he* was scaring *her*. What was it Muriel said once? *People's indifference is the most frightening thing of all.*

Brett turned around and locked eyes with her. "And I don't want you to give that speech, either," he said.

Chloe's chin hit the ground. Her smoldering anger was about to erupt when Brett took her hands and added tenderly, "I love you, Chloe. I couldn't stand it if anything ever happened to you. I mean that. I don't want to tell you how to think or how to be. I don't care if you're a vegetarian for *the movement,*" he drew out the words. "Believe whatever you want. Just don't put yourself at risk anymore. Don't be such a fanatic. Every minute of every day I worry about what crazy stunt you'll pull next. And if you're going to get hurt. I can't live this way."

"But—"

He pressed a finger to her lips. "That speech is a good example. There are a lot of people mad about this law, fighting mad. Don't you watch the news?"

Chloe tried to open her mouth to answer.

Before she could utter a sound, he added. "Oh, I forgot. You don't have a TV. Well, you should see these guys they're interviewing. I mean, some of them are ready to kill. And it's not just ranchers. These are like medical researchers, people at university labs, animal breeders. My dad, for instance, says he'll lose a big development contract for the new P & M food and drug factory. They won't build here when most of their products are banned. A lot of people need those jobs. This is a hot issue, Chloe. And there you are with your picture plastered all over the front page of the newspaper. 'Local girl speaking on behalf of animal rights at legislative hearing,'" he recited.

Chloe blushed. "That was Muriel's idea. I didn't

have anything to do with that story. I mean, she didn't have to put in all that stuff about how I won the Junior Humanitarian Award when I was seven. Or how I got my elementary school to start serving vegetarian meals when I was nine. Or how I rescued Deaf Leopard from a dumpster. Besides, it was just the *Transcript*. Who reads that rag?"

Brett continued as if he hadn't heard her. "I don't want you caught in the middle of this war, especially up on the front lines. Believe in it, okay. Just don't get involved. Please. For me. For us."

He pulled her close and held her hard against him. The inner turmoil of her conflicting emotions suddenly burst apart. She trembled. She wished she could cry, but she didn't feel like crying. More like punching. Fighting. Strangling.

For a long time they stood there together: Chloe, struggling to understand, to stay composed; and Brett, seemingly battling to maintain his composure too, while the growing shadow of Buffalo Bill engulfed them.

Chloe squeezed her eyes shut. *I don't want to lose him,* she thought.

Brett loosened his grip on her. He tilted her chin up and gazed into her eyes. "Tell you what," he said, brushing his fingers along her cheek. "You don't have to decide right now, but if you'll do this for me, I'll do something for you. I'll stop eating meat." He squinched. "At least I'll try. Is that fair?"

"Fair?" She inhaled a deep breath, exhaled, and gazed out over his head. A star flickered momentarily, then disappeared in the clouds. Without looking at him, she said, "Haven't you heard? Life isn't fair."

The sun had set by the time Chloe and Brett turned onto Chloe's street. It was almost too dark to see. Almost. "Hey, Chloe," Brett said, "there's a police car parked in your driveway. I wonder what's going on."

She squinted down the block. Actually, there were two vehicles in the driveway. The other was an ambulance.

chocolate and served it to her at the dining-room table. Chloe drank half of it before she realized what it was. "Did you put milk in this?" she asked.

"Oops. Yeah, I did. Sorry." He bent down to retrieve the mug. "I wasn't thinking. Do you want something else?"

Chloe shook her head. She took the mug back from him, lifted it to her lips, and finished it all.

Chloe wandered through the next week in a daze. If she let herself feel, for even an instant, she knew she'd never make it through the day.

But sometimes the grief broke free. She grieved for all the other stolen animals, all their owners. They'd never know what happened to their beloved family pets. If they suffered or died. If they were used for some painful experiment, then just disposed of. It made her sick. The only peace of mind Chloe found was in sleep, so she crawled into bed as soon as she got home from school every day and stayed there.

On Thursday night, Chloe woke with a start. Through the floorboards, she heard her grandmother's alarm clock chime midnight. She rolled over in bed and pulled the panda over her face. Chloe squeezed her eyes shut, trying to recapture the numbness of sleep.

Suddenly there was a sound at the door, a soft mewing. "Deaf?" Chloe threw off the panda and opened her eyes. She froze. "Gran." She sat up. "What are you doing here?"

Chapter 16

Chloe and Brett raced to her house. When they got there, Chloe's father and a police officer were standing in the foyer speaking in lowered voices. Her father's face looked strained.

"What's happened, Dad?"

When he didn't answer, a horrible thought gripped Chloe. "Oh, no. Where's Gran?"

Her father caught her arm on her way past him to Gran's bedroom. "She's all right," he said. "Dr. Shaeffer came. He gave her a sedative. She's not hurt, Chloe. Not physically."

She felt a rush of relief spread through her already weary body. Her father drew Chloe in with an arm around her shoulders, and she slumped against him. In the doorframe, Brett mimed, "I'll call you later." He backed out.

The officer said, "Lucky for you the manager

at Bird Boutique isn't going to press charges, Dr. Mankewicz. But he was tempted, let me tell you. Especially since he'd already had one run-in with a Mankewicz." He eyed Chloe.

Her cheeks flared. "What's he talking about, Dad? What happened?"

"I'll tell you later," he replied, eyes glued to the officer.

"Is your mother under a psychiatrist's care?" the officer asked.

"I don't think that's any of your business." Dr. Mankewicz glanced down at the officer's report. "Sergeant Carello. I appreciate you bringing her home. Will that be all?"

The officer shrugged. He closed his notebook, turned, and left. Latching the door behind him, Chloe's father sighed audibly. He said to the ceiling, "I need a drink."

"Dad?"

"Tea. Strong tea." He smiled vaguely and headed for the kitchen. Chloe followed.

"They found her skulking up and down the aisles, tearing into fifty pound bags of wild bird feed. She was mumbling something about Colombian stash." Chloe's father filled the teapot and set it on the stove. "I think she was looking for coffee."

"Da-ad." Chloe whapped his arm.

"Do you have any idea why she would have worn her pajamas outside the house?"

Chloe lowered her eyes. "I didn't tell you. I

didn't want you to worry. She forgets sometimes how to dress herself."

"What?"

"I usually get up early to help her, but I was in such a hurry this morning . . ." Chloe blinked up at him. "Sorry, Dad. It won't happen again."

He shook his head. "Don't apologize. You should've told me about this. What else?"

Chloe frowned. "Nothing. That's it."

"Chloe?" The teapot whistled. He lifted it off the burner and turned off the gas. Then he poured the hot water over his metal tea ball and carried the cup to the dining room. Chloe trailed, shaking a can of V8.

"Dr. Shaeffer said Mother was pretty agitated and incoherent," Chloe's father continued, sitting down at the table. "He recommended . . ." He exhaled. "Maybe it's time to—"

"Ship her off to a nursing home?" Chloe finished his sentence. "No." She took her seat across from him.

"It's not a nursing home. It's an elder-care facility. They specialize in this type of—of illness. They have a resident medical staff, trained caregivers."

"I can take care of her," Chloe said. "I have been for years. In fact, I was going to quit the shelter so I could spend more time at home." Chloe was shocked by her own statement. When had she decided that? Had Brett's paranoia, his worry over her safety, forced her decision? *No,* she answered herself. *Of course not. It's my deci-*

sion. In fact, quitting the shelter is the only solu-
tion. Gran needs me.

"After school, too," Chloe added. "Brett and I'll be coming here from now on."

"Oh?" He studied her over the rim of his cup.

A smile tugged the corners of her lips. "I'm going to teach him how to be a vegetarian."

"How'd you manage that?" he asked, immediately answering, "Never mind. I have succumbed to the Chloe Mankewicz power of persuasion myself. Except in this case. Your mother was right—it isn't fair to expect you to take care of your grandmother. Especially if she's deteriorating as fast as you say."

"Dad, it's not that bad. If I'm willing to do it—"

He held up a hand. "I've already agreed to visit this Meridian Care Center tomorrow with Dr. Shaeffer. Why don't you come along? Maybe you'll change your mind." His eyes strayed to the French doors and, gazing out unseeing into the thickening night, he added wearily, "Maybe I'll change my mind."

The sadness in her father's voice forced Chloe to retreat, for now. Reluctantly she nodded okay, although she knew it was pointless for her to visit this place. Nothing was going to change her mind.

"What time is Thanksgiving on Thursday?" Her father changed the subject. "Did your mother say?"

Chloe shrugged. "One or two." *Thanks for reminding me,* she said to herself. *Another item to*

*add to my list of "Things Most Dreaded." That,
along with informing Muriel Blevins that the for-
mer activist Chloe Mankewicz could no longer be
the voice of youth for the movement. Muriel was
right,* Chloe thought. *I am a love slave.*

Chloe skipped her classes Monday morning to
go with her father, grandmother, and Dr. Shaeffer to the Meridian Care Center. The tour re-
minded Chloe how she'd felt the last time she'd
visited the zoo. The animals were alive, yet life-
less. They wandered around with nothing to do
but wait for mealtime. "Survival of the fattest,"
Chloe called it. Her heart ached as the elderly
residents at the care center filled the cafeteria
tables for lunch. It wasn't even ten o'clock.

"It's a state-of-the-art facility," Dr. Shaeffer
said. "There's an in-house beauty shop and phar-
macy. The reading room is over there, behind the
big-screen TV." He pointed.

Chloe saw her father flinch.

The doctor continued, "Your mother'd be shar-
ing an apartment with another lady about her
age."

Chloe hated how he talked about Gran as if
she wasn't there.

He added in a lowered voice, "Usually there's
a waiting list, but you're in luck. A bed freed up
yesterday."

Chloe said, "Who died?"

Her grandmother tightened her grip on
Chloe's arm.

120

"No one died." Dr. Shaeffer smiled down at her. "The woman was moved to another section of the facility where she'll get more immediate medical attention."

"You mean the psycho ward?"

"Chloe." Her father frowned a warning.

"I'm sorry, Dad. I can't take this." She broke free of Gran and bolted for the parking lot. It was all happening too fast. Gran could never survive in a place like this. *That's not true,* Chloe corrected herself. *She could survive, but she could never live. And there's a world of difference.*

The doctor and Chloe's father came out a few minutes later with Gran shackled between them. Dr. Shaeffer looked tense.

"What happened?" Chloe asked as her father helped Gran into the front seat.

"We only turned our backs for a minute." Dr. Mankewicz fastened the seat belt around his mother. "Somehow your grandmother found the loudspeaker and announced to the whole place that the Air Alitalia flight they were on was being hijacked to Hanoi."

Chapter 17

At home, after settling Gran in for a nap, Chloe sat down with her father in the living room. "At least wait until after Thanksgiving to make a decision about Gran," she said.

He sighed wearily and rubbed his eyes behind his glasses.

"Come on, Dad. It's only a week. Moving Gran now would ruin the holidays—for everyone." It was a low blow, she knew that, but this was desperation time.

He rested his head against the back of the chair. "She can't be left alone. I'm sorry, Chloe."

Chloe wracked her brain. "Wasn't there a volunteer service at the nursing home—I mean, the facility? Didn't they have people who'd come in to check up on patients in their homes? Make sure they took their medicine and stuff? We could try that first."

He arched a hopeful eyebrow. "I think you're right. I'll give Dr. Shaeffer a call. It's only a temporary solution, though, Chloe. You know that."

Right, she told herself. *But in a week he'll forget all about moving her. He'll see how unnecessary the move is, how much happier and safer Gran is at home. How I can be relied on to take care of her. A week is a long time. Seven whole days.*

Thanksgiving day began as expected. Chloe's mother flitted around her condo in a pink satin jumpsuit, fussing over the hors d'oeuvres and drinks. The first surprise came when the bell buzzed and a strange man appeared. "This is Juan." Chloe's mother linked her arm in his. "Juan is my Latin dance instructor."

"Olé." Juan snapped his fingers.

Chloe didn't join her mother in the laughter. "What happened to Roger?" she said.

Her mother's spine went rigid. In a cold voice, she answered, "He found someone else. A playmate about your age. Help yourself to hors d'oeuvres, Juan. I'll fix you a drink." She headed for the kitchen.

Chloe blanched. She thought, *Open mouth, insert hoof.* She followed her mother through the cafe doors to apologize, but before she could say a word, her mother handed her a set of tongs and said, "Would you mind tossing the salad, dear?"

Chloe flipped greens while her mother poured wine for Juan and took it to him. When she returned, she taste-tested the gravy over the stove. Although the smell of burning turkey flesh began to roil Chloe's stomach, she closed her nostrils and bit her tongue. "You look pretty today," her mother said.

Was that retaliation, round one? Chloe wondered. She scanned her own outfit, from the blood-red rubber boots on her feet to the high-button collar of her black mourning dress. She thought, *I should have worn my "Only Turkeys Eat Turkey" T-shirt.*

Her mother fluttered false eyelashes at her and smiled. "Are you wearing makeup?"

Chloe cheeks flared. She dropped her eyes. "Cruelty-free. Aveda."

"Cruelty-free?" her mother repeated. "I didn't know there was such a thing."

Chloe looked at her. "There are lots of ethical, responsible product-makers, Mother."

"It's not just the makeup," she said. "You seem different. Softer. More feminine. It's Brett, isn't it? I already like him. So when am I going to meet him?"

Never, Chloe answered in her mind. *Not in this life.* Her eyes darted around the shrinking room, searching for the nearest exit. Before Chloe could escape, her mother added, "Oh, there's a spinach soufflé in the oven for you, darling. Would you take a peek at it?" She sipped from her champagne goblet and returned attention to the stove.

"A soufflé?" Chloe repeated. "Aren't those made

with eggs?" She peered in through the tinted glass oven doors.

When she looked back at her mother, she gulped. All the makeup in the Desiree dominion couldn't have masked her mother's rankling. "I've, uh, decided to become a vegan," Chloe said feebly. "No eggs or dairy products."

Her mother began to stir the gravy mercilessly. *You idiot,* Chloe scolded herself. Her mother was trying, she really was. "I could start next week. I mean, this soufflé looks fantastic."

Chloe's eyes met her mother's. There was actually a current of warmth between them. Chloe thought she'd extend the moment by informing her mother of her decision not to become involved in the animal rights legislation when her father unexpectedly appeared.

"My mother and your boyfriend are in the living room conspiring to overthrow the government of Brazil. Any plans in here to maybe carve up Turkey?" He chomped on a carrot stick.

Chloe and her mother groaned in unison.

After school on Monday, Chloe waited to walk home with Muriel. She couldn't put off the dreaded announcement any longer. She had to tell her. The legislative committee meeting was Friday. It had been an agonizing decision to drop the speech. On the one hand Chloe resented Brett for asking her, yet on the other he was making sacrifices for the sake of their relationship, too. By becoming a vegetarian, he was honoring her wishes. Wasn't it selfish for Chloe not to do the same? The speech was just a big ego trip anyway. Wasn't it? Well, wasn't it?

"Muriel, about the speech—"

"Oh, Chloe. I'm so glad you brought it up," Muriel said. "I was beginning to think you'd forgotten or, forgive me for even thinking this, lost interest." They made tracks in the mud along the front of the football bleachers. From the far side of the field, Brett waved to Chloe as she and Muriel headed for home.

Brett had a special practice every day after school this week to prepare for the play-off game on Saturday. Or so he said. Chloe suspected he was avoiding coming to her house because of Gran. She'd begun to frisk him at the door. Either that, or he'd OD'd on oat bran.

"I apologize," Muriel said. "Of course it's ridiculous to think you would've lost interest. It is the movement, after all. I know you've been distracted by this situation with your grandmother. Not to mention what's-his-worship."

Chloe gave her a dirty look. Muriel missed it because she was rummaging in her bookbag for something. "I'd never question the strength of your convictions, Chloe. Never. Sometimes I just question my own. Like when my mother refuses to allow me to give up milk and eggs to become a vegan." Muriel sighed. "It isn't fair."

Inwardly Chloe blanched. "Life isn't fair sometimes, Muriel," she said. "For instance—"

"No sense crying over spilled milk," Muriel cut

her off. "Anyway, look what I found." She flipped open her notebook and brushed through the pages. "Here it is. Did you know that only ten percent of all medical advances can be attributed to animal research?"

"No, I didn't, Mur. What I was saying—" Chloe stopped short. "Ten percent? Is that all?"

"And the number of repeat experiments is staggering. You know, experiments that are conducted over and over again because one scientist doesn't know what the others are doing? For example, isolation tests where animal babies are taken from their mothers at birth. They've been repeated two hundred times. Infecting animals with diabetes, eleven hundred times. Oh, and this will make your blood boil. Tests for radiation cancer have been repeated thirty-eight thousand times."

"Thirty-eight thousand times? The same test?"

Muriel nodded. "Horrifying, isn't it? This law is so important. Think of all the unnecessary suffering it'll prevent." She turned to Chloe and said, "We should include these statistics in the speech, don't you think?"

They'd reached the end of Chloe's driveway by then. Chloe said, "Statistics work better on paper, Mur. The most effective speeches appeal to people's emotions."

"You're right. Of course you're right. That's why you're doing this and not me." Muriel grinned.

Chloe lowered her head and plowed toward the

porch. *Oh, man. What am I saying?* she wondered. *Am I giving this speech, or not?* She spun to face Muriel. Standing there bathed in the glow of Muriel's adulation, a spark of the old Chloe fire reignited. She felt the adrenalin pumping through her veins, the passion surging. *I can't,* she caught herself. *I just can't.*

Muriel smiled admiring eyes. Chloe made a decision. "Do you still have that report you wrote on why you converted to vegetarianism? You know, the one about the nightmares you had after watching that documentary on the chicken ranch where they debeak the chickens so they won't peck each other? I really thought it captured the spirit of the movement."

"You did? Oh, Chloe, do you really want to use it? I'd be honored."

I must be insane, Chloe thought. *Brett's going to kill me. No, he'll be upset, maybe even a little angry, but he'll understand. This'll be the last time, I'll promise him. Besides, who else could possibly be the voice of youth?* "So, how's the bio bond between you and Mr. Keifer these days?" Chloe asked, taking the speech notes from Muriel.

Muriel scoffed. "That fat fool? Do you know he had the gall to give me a B+ on my lab work? And I found out he expects us to dissect pigs for our final. I suggested we dissect him; it'd give us more corpse to work with."

Chloe laughed. "Oh, Mur. I've missed you." She slugged Muriel's arm. She reached for the doorknob and stopped. It wasn't there. Or rather, the knob wasn't where she expected it to be, because the front door was hanging wide open.

"Gran?" Chloe called, stepping inside.

Silence. Where was she? Where was the volunteer who was supposed to be here with her? Something else was wrong, too.

Chloe stomped her foot. "Deaf?"

"What's this?" Muriel stooped to pick up a sheet of paper off the foyer floor.

They both read the note aloud, "Through animal research we have the power to heal disease and spare the suffering of thousands, maybe millions. We are the moral species. We must not allow legislation of animal rights to supersede human rights. Animals were put on this earth to be the servants of man. They must be sacrificed in order to serve the ultimate good."

"Oh, brother," Chloe said. "Someone's been distributing these flyers all over town. Brett showed me one he got yesterday."

"I know," Muriel said. "Angela Herrera told me she's getting a lot of calls about animals being stolen out of people's yards."

"Really?" Chloe noticed some writing on the back. "There's more." She turned the sheet over.

She and Muriel read the scrawled P.S. "Thank you for your donation."

"My donation? What—" Chloe's stomach lurched. She breathed, "Oh, my God. Deaf!"

Chapter 18

Chloe shot up the stairs with Muriel at her heels. She threw open her bedroom door and yelled, "Deaf! Deaf!" She stomped her feet. Her heart pounded in her throat. He wasn't in his usual sleeping place, curled up in her giant panda. "Deaf," she whispered hoarsely.

Nothing. No sound. Then something. A scratching. Chloe's eyes were drawn to the sound. Her closet door was closed, which was odd. She never closed it. Muriel reached the closet first and forced the door open.

"Deaf!" they both cried in unison.

The sleepy cat stretched and yawned. Chloe snatched him up in her arms. Tears of joy, of relief, clouded her vision.

"Thank goodness he's safe," Muriel said. She kissed Deaf's head. A sound, a sort of scuffling came from downstairs.

Then Chloe remembered. "Gran?" she called.

Cuddling Deaf close, she scurried back down the stairs. Her father stood in the foyer, his arm wrapped around Gran's shoulder. She huddled, trembling inside an old army blanket. Someone else was with them.

"Thank you, Sergeant Carello," Dr. Mankewicz said. "I appreciate you bringing us home."

Chloe waited until the officer left before she asked, "Dad, what happened?"

"Gran went out," he said flatly.

Chloe bit her lip. "Is she all right? Where was she?"

"She's fine," he answered, ushering Gran toward her room. "Hello, Muriel. Do you mind if Chloe and I talk?"

"Not at all, Dr. Mankewicz." Muriel backed toward the door. "I'll call you later, Chloe. We can finish the speech tomorrow."

"Okay, Mur. Thanks. Thanks for everything."

Muriel gave Deaf another kiss on the head and squeezed Chloe's hand before leaving.

"Dad, it's my fault—"

Her father held up a hand. "Could you put on some hot water? I need to get Mom to bed."

Chloe hustled to the kitchen. She set Deaf on the counter and commanded, "Stay." *If only he were a dog,* she thought. *A big, vicious dog.* She decided she'd never let Deaf out of her sight. Never.

As she carried the tea to the dining room, she met her father coming in. "Gran was gone when

I got home, Dad," Chloe said. "I don't know where the volunteer was—"

"Sit down, Chloe." He pulled her chair out for her.

"I have another solution, Dad. I know we don't have room for a live-in, but we could hire a full-time caregiver, maybe even a college student, to stay during the day—"

"It costs too much. I've already looked into it." Her father took a deep breath. "Your grandmother was found at your school wandering the halls, calling your name. For her own protection, and my peace of mind, I think it's time we faced reality. I've decided to move her to Meridian this weekend."

"Dad, no! We can take care of her. There's got to be a way."

"We'll talk about your grandmother later. There's something else we need to discuss." He stood from his chair across from her and retrieved his briefcase. Pulling out a stack of envelopes, he said, "That news story about you may not have been such a great idea. I've been getting notes in my mailbox at school. Threatening notes." He handed her a stack.

Chloe read the top sheet. It was the flyer, the same flyer she found in the foyer, and on the back was a scribbled note: "Tell your daughter to back off." The next one said, "Control your daughter or else." Chloe shuddered.

Her father took the stack back, and said, "I'm not sure what 'or else' means, but—"

Chloe cut him off, "It means they're coming to take Deaf."

"What?"

She removed the crumpled flyer from her back pocket and showed him.

"Where'd you find this?"

"On the floor. In the front hall." She pointed.

"In our house? They were in our house? How'd they get in?" He stopped. He met Chloe's eyes. Suddenly the cafe doors whooshed open and Gran scuttled in. She was naked except for the army blanket. She clutched Chloe's arm and wheezed, "Death squad."

Chloe met her father's eyes. He was right. Gran was gone.

Hours later, when she'd thought everything through, Chloe knew what she had to do. There was no choice now. She called Muriel first.

"It's all my fault," Muriel said. "I shouldn't have written that article."

"No, Mur," Chloe replied. "They would've found out somehow. Everyone involved in this bill is getting harassed. Anyway," she inhaled a long, trembling breath, "I can't give the speech. I can't be the voice of youth. I'm too afraid they'll try to steal Deaf again. The thought of him being sold to a research lab is just too horrible to imagine." Her voice cracked. "And I can't trust Gran to . . ." Chloe began to cry.

Muriel sniffled. "I understand, Chloe," she said. "Don't worry. I'll take care of it."

Chloe called Brett next. She was so upset she could hardly speak. Somehow she managed to tell him everything that had happened.

"I'm coming over," Brett said.

"No, you don't have to."

"I know I don't have to. I want to. I want to be with you."

She was so glad to have Brett. So glad.

When he got to her house, Brett said, "Let's take a walk."

Chloe shut Deaf in her room before she left. "Don't move," she warned him. He perched atop her stereo speaker, washing his whiskers, oblivious to any danger.

Chloe and Brett headed toward Grisham Park. "This never would've happened if they'd known you already decided not to give that speech," Brett said. He sat down on Buffalo Bill's boot. "Oh, Chloe. I'm sorry." He smoothed her hair back from her tortured face, and held her.

She didn't tell him the truth. What was the use? She wasn't going to give the speech now, anyway. They stood like that for a long time. How long, Chloe couldn't say. She'd lost track of time. The wind blew dust devils at their feet. Someone had knocked over a trash can, and a Styrofoam hamburger carton bounced by them on its way to the frozen lake. Chloe shivered.

"Let's go," Brett said. "It's too cold out here."

Chloe didn't feel cold. She didn't feel anything. She let him take her hand and lead her away.

Back at her house, Brett warmed some hot

"Chloe? Is that you?" Her grandmother hunched in the doorway. She shaded her eyes against the wash of moonlight from Chloe's bay window. Shuffling in, she closed the door behind her and perched on the edge of Chloe's bed.

"You're in my room, Gran," Chloe said wearily. "Come on, I'll take you back downstairs." She swung her legs out from under the covers.

"Warning. I must deliver this warning," her grandmother whispered urgently, grasping Chloe by the knee. "They have infiltrated the hideout. They are approaching. The enemy is within."

Chloe sighed. She loosened her grandmother's grip and stood up before her, tugging gently on her hands.

Gran locked eyes with her. "They broke in. I couldn't stop them. They looked for him, your Deaf. I hid him in your closet. I had to find you, to warn you."

Chloe frowned a little and sat down next to her grandmother. "Is that why you came to the school, Gran? To warn me?"

Her grandmother's eyes widened with panic, yet they seemed clear and lucid to Chloe. "I tried to stop them," she said. "I couldn't hold the door. I tried. I tried. . . ." She lowered her head. Her voice trailed off in a whimper.

Chloe wrapped an arm around her grandmother's shoulders and squeezed gently. "Oh, Gran. I didn't even think about them breaking in. It must have been terrifying for you. I'm sorry. I'm sure you tried to stop them." She rested her head on her grandmother's bony shoulder. "I'm sorry for everything," she said softly, tears filling her eyes. "Especially for giving up on you. But, Gran, you saved Deaf. See?" She lifted her cat off the pillow and showed her grandmother.

"They won't take me. The infiltrators will never take me alive." Her grandmother whipped her head up. Chloe saw the all-too-familiar glazed look reappear. "Capture is imminent. Death is the only means of escape. A noble death." She clutched Chloe's knee between her icy fingers. "Don't let them take me. I beg you, Carlos." She ended in a stream of incoherent babble.

Chloe took her grandmother back to her own bed. Tucking her in, she kissed her goodnight, then whispered, "I won't let them take you, Gran. Not ever."

Chapter 19

Chloe curled onto her window seat and rested her chin on her knees. Her eyes were drawn to the walls, illuminated in the pink glow of early dawn—her walls, papered with posters of endangered species, each one a haunting reminder of the past. The past. It all seemed so distant now. So long ago. Her dream of making a difference, of saving just one species from extinction, one animal from the suffering or humiliation caused by human exploitation.

"They're in danger," she heard herself say. "All of them. Dead or dying. Their habitats destroyed." She stared into the eyes of the Florida panther. Eyes the color of Deaf's. Trusting eyes. Beautiful eyes. Chloe crumpled over her knees. *I can't let what they've done to you, to all of you, go on like this,* she thought. *It has to stop.* She raised her head. Brett's words came back to her. "Believe in it, okay. Just don't get involved."

"It won't stop by wishing it away, Brett," she said, as if he were in the room. "Nothing will change by simply believing." She scanned the room. "I won't give up on you. I promise. Somebody has to *do* something. Me. *I* have to. I'm sorry, Brett. But believing isn't enough. Not for me."

Muriel had already left her house when Chloe called the next morning. As she was hanging up the phone, her father wandered into the kitchen, shoving a stack of test papers into his backpack. "Morning, Dad," she said, pecking him on the cheek.

"Chloe." He stopped abruptly. "You seem . . . happy. Have you gone off the deep end?"

"Glub, glub. What you're hearing is the voice of youth," she replied.

He raised an eyebrow. "You're giving the speech today? Are you sure about this?" he asked.

"Sure? I've never been more sure of anything in my life. Power to the pigs!" She plunged her fist in the air.

Her father chuckled. "I didn't figure anyone had the power to silence the voice of youth."

She made a face at him. "I just hate locking Deaf in my room every day."

"I talked to the police," he said, "and told them about the threatening letters. They said they'd keep an eye on the house. I don't think you need to worry about Deaf."

"Thanks, Dad." Chloe kissed his cheek. "Maybe we could get a couple of extra locks, too. Dead bolts that lock from the inside, for Gran."

"Chloe, about Gran . . ."

She grabbed a granola bar from the cupboard. "Don't do anything about Gran until we talk about it some more, okay?"

In a soft voice, he said, "I already decided."

She whirled on him. "*You* decided. What about me?"

He held her eyes. "I think you know this is the only solution. I hate doing it. I hate the thought of giving up on her. But honey, we lost her a long time ago. She's only going to get more forgetful, more . . ." He swallowed hard. "This is the best way. The only way." He turned away from her.

She felt her throat constricting. As much as she wanted to deny it, she knew he was right. She knew. Oh, Gran.

The sound of the doorbell made them both jump. Chloe blinked back her tears and grabbed her bag. In the hallway, her grandmother hurtled out of her room wielding a hairbrush. Chloe stopped and hugged her. "Sub rosa," she whispered in her grandmother's ear.

"The serpent returns," her grandmother whispered back.

Chloe hissed. It wouldn't be the same without Gran. She felt as if she were losing a part of herself—more and more of herself. . . .

Brett's finger was poised to ring the doorbell again when Chloe flung open the front door. "Hi," he said. He scanned her once, twice, three times. "What are you wearing?" he finally said.

She straightened the turban on her head. "These are fightin' duds, dude. You got your 'Abolish Animal Slavery' T-shirt," she held her coat open, "your 'Animal Lib' button, 'Wail for the Whales' stickers, and oh, yeah, 'Stop Species-ism' banner." She pulled the rolled-up cloth out of her bag and unfurled it over the porch rail.

"You look like you're going to—"

Chloe met his eyes. "Would you like to ride the bus with me downtown? Ditch school for the day?"

He didn't answer. Instead, he focused on a spot over her head across the frozen lawn to the empty street, and beyond. When he gazed down at her again, he said, "I can't, Chloe. I love you too much."

Her spine stiffened. She felt the anger rising up the back of her neck. "No, you don't," she said. All those months of pent-up emotions suddenly burst through the dam. "You don't love me, Brett. You love the person you want me to be."

With an electric jolt of reality, she realized that what she'd said was true. She'd known it for a long time now, she just didn't want to admit it. Just like she didn't want to admit a lot of things. He didn't love the real Chloe Mankewicz. He didn't even know her. He loved that she was different. Interesting. But he must've thought it was an act. Chloe had given up her identity for him. Now she felt afraid. Afraid of where this revelation was leading.

"It's not your fault, Brett," she added hastily. "I mean, I'm the one who changed."

"Yeah. You sure did," he replied coolly. Without another word, he turned on his heel and stalked off toward school.

She wanted to call out to him, to make him stop. But his name stuck in her throat and she could only manage a hoarse whisper. "Brett. Don't go."

At the corner, he sprinted across the street and disappeared in a blur. Commanding all her strength to stanch an avalanche of tears, Chloe took off running for the bus stop. The downtown express was just pulling away from the curb when she arrived, out of breath and wheezing. She slumped onto the bench to wait for the next bus.

Chloe fought to erase the image of Brett running away. What was going to happen between them? Would he still love her after this? Would he accept her the way she really was? Did she love *him?* Maybe that was the real question.

She'd have to reconcile her feelings about Brett, about Gran, about everything. But not today. Today was for the animals. "I wonder what Muriel did about the speech," she thought out loud. "I hope she didn't cancel it."

Chloe didn't notice the car pulling up at the

curb. It was the hum of an electric window scrolling down that made her glance up. "I thought that was you. Would you like a ride to the capitol, darling?" her mother said. "It's on my way."

Chapter 20

"Let me off a couple of blocks away, Mother," Chloe said, fastening her seat belt. "I don't want to be seen driving up in this car."

Her mother smiled vaguely. She glanced into the sideview mirror before merging the lavender Lexus out into traffic. With a sigh, she said, "Yes, my trophy on wheels. I suppose I'll have to give up my chariot when I leave the company."

Chloe widened her eyes at her. "You're quitting Desiree?"

"Well, I'm glad your first inclination wasn't to ask if I was fired. Yes, as of yesterday, I am no longer the Western Regional Director for Desiree Cosmetics, Inc." She swerved between two buses to change lanes, then slammed on her brakes behind a stalled car.

Chloe, bouncing off the padded dashboard, said, "So, what are you going to do?"

Her mother lifted her rose-tinted sunglasses and smooshed them into her hair. "Remember at Thanksgiving, when I noticed how pretty you looked with makeup? You mentioned the products you use are, how did you put it, crueltyless?"

"Cruelty-free," Chloe said, blushing at the compliment.

"That's right, cruelty-free. Well, that started me thinking. I've been noticing how this movement of yours is catching on. All this sudden social consciousness to save the planet."

Not so sudden, Mother, Chloe thought. *You've just been living in Barbie's dream world.*

They lurched out into traffic again, brakes squealing. Chloe thought, *I'm going to lose my breakfast.* "So, you're joining up?" she said, wondering how upchucked granola would go with purple upholstery.

"Do I have a choice?" her mother answered. "Let's just say I'm positioning myself for the opportunities available for someone with my unique talents."

Chloe wanted to laugh. She restrained herself, but her mother must've noticed. She pressed on the gas pedal. "I've been hired as a beauty consultant at the Palm Springs Health Resort and Spa," she said. "It's basically a fat farm, but the overindulgent deserve to feel beautiful—for a week, at least."

A sudden warmth spread through Chloe. She

was feeling benevolent today, thankful for any stability in her life. Even her mother. Then the words struck her. "Palm Springs? As in California?"

"I'm not deserting you," her mother added quickly. "We'll see each other on holidays and in summers. Probably more than we do now."

Chloe felt a twinge of regret, which lingered, suprisingly. "Couldn't you find something closer? Something here in town?"

Her mother blinked across at her. A car horn blared, and she blinked back. "I guess I could keep looking. If it means that much to you."

Chloe bit her lip.

Her mother reached across and squeezed Chloe's hand. She slammed on the brakes again and cursed the taxi in front of them, bringing the magic moment to an abrupt halt.

"Well, here we are." Chloe's mother pulled into a reserved parking space at the curb across the street from the state capitol building. "Good luck on your speech. By the way, how's Brett?"

Chloe blanched. As she opened the door, she swallowed hard and said, "Don't ask."

Her mother frowned. "Oh, darling." She tilted her head. "I'm sorry. Maybe we can have lunch next week and talk about it. I'm an expert on exes." She arched both eyebrows.

Exes. It sounded so final. Chloe's stomach knotted. She perched on the edge of the seat for a moment, then looked back over her shoulder and thought, *I really do need someone to talk to.* "Thanks, Mom," Chloe said. "I'll call you."

The schedule board said the animal rights legislation hearing was slated to begin at 9:00 in room 312. Chloe searched the labyrinth of hallways until she found the room. The double doors were closed with a sign that said, "In Session." Chloe checked her watch. 10:08. Inside, she heard the muted voice of a speaker. No guards were around, so she pulled on the handle and tiptoed in.

The speaker was finishing an announcement. "That was Mary Stimpson from PETA, People for the Ethical Treatment of Animals. Thank you, Mary."

Chloe felt a tug on her coat sleeve. Glancing down, she found Angela motioning Chloe into the empty seat next to her on the aisle. Chloe slid in, whispering, "Where's Muriel?"

Before Angela could reply, the announcer said, "Our next speaker was selected by the Humane Society to represent the voice of youth." Someone tapped the speaker on the shoulder. He held his hand over the microphone while a message was relayed. "There's been a change," he told the audience, jotting on his program notes. "The voice of youth will be represented by Miss Muriel Blevins."

"What?" Chloe whipped her head around to stare at Angela.

Angela smiled. "She volunteered."

Chloe looked back. Muriel rose from her chair at the back of the stage and approached the microphone. "Hooboy. She's really going to do it," Chloe thought out loud.

Muriel tapped her notecards on the lectern and cleared her throat. "L-l-l-adies and g-g-g-gentlemen," she began.

Chloe winced. She could feel Muriel's panic.

Muriel swallowed hard and began again. "Ladies and gentlemen. My friend C-Chloe Mankewicz was supposed to give this speech today." Muriel's voice shook like Jell-O. "Believe it or n-not, she's a much better public speaker than I am." Her pained expression sparked a current of laughter throughout the audience.

"Chloe's the most dedicated, outspoken, committed animal rights activist you could ever know. If she were here today, I know you'd feel assured that the animals of the earth will be protected in the future." Muriel paused and drew a deep, trembling breath. "But she's not here, and I'll tell you why. The people who wanted her out of this assembly—the same people who believe animals were put on this planet to serve us—these *people* broke into Chloe's house and tried to steal her eleven-year-old deaf cat to sell to a medical laboratory."

As cries of outrage filled the committee room, Chloe felt her own tears welling up again. She lowered her head and breathed deeply to rein them in. Angela squeezed her hand in her lap.

"Thankfully they didn't get her cat, but they

threatened to try again. I'd like to address those people now," Muriel continued, her voice still quivering. "Congratulations. You succeeded in eliminating Chloe. Now, what are your plans for silencing the rest of us?"

A rally of spontaneous applause erupted. Chloe looked around. There must've been two hundred people in the audience; lots of people her age, and even younger.

Chloe didn't hear the rest of Muriel's speech. She didn't have to. She watched its effect on the room as people reached out to clasp hands in a gesture of strength and unity. Muriel's words, though fluttery to the end, inspired a standing ovation. Chloe clapped the loudest. She stomped her feet. In the end, she just couldn't help herself. In her most resonant contralto, she began the chant, "Give life a chance. Give life a chance."

The people around her all linked arms and began to sway. They joined in her appeal. Tears clouded Chloe's eyes, but they were tears of joy and she welcomed them. She watched Muriel shake hands with Governor Eicher, and with the president of PETA. Chloe bit her lip. Those could've been her handshakes, her moment of glory. *No,* Chloe told herself. *This is Muriel's victory. She was there when it counted. She never wavered in her convictions. She never let anything, or anyone, change her.*

Chloe was so proud of Muriel. And so ashamed of herself. Through the tears, she felt a warmth inside her core begin to spread, and she knew that this was where she belonged. This was home. Here, among these people, where something mattered. Where Chloe Mankewicz, one small, insignificant human being on the planet, could make a difference. Could make it better. *Yes,* she thought. *I'm back. And I'm stronger than ever.* She smiled to herself. "Look out, world."

Chapter 21

"The bill passed the committee, and now it's headed for the house," Muriel said. She peeled back her carton of yogurt. "They'll be voting on it after Christmas break. Keep your fingers crossed."

Chloe said, "Keep everything crossed." She crossed her eyes at Muriel and they both cracked up.

"So, how's your grandmother doing?" Muriel asked.

Chloe finished her sandwich and folded the foil in fourths. "Better than expected. When the other residents at Meridian found out she was a CIA operative, they were in awe. She's a celebrity."

Muriel arched an eyebrow. "But—"

"Yeah, I know. She worked for two weeks as a Merry Maid. Don't tell her that."

Muriel laughed. From her bookbag she pulled

out a red folder, and said, "Mr. Keifer agreed to moderate the panel on Friday. I guess he's not so bad. Although he's probably on the pro side." She curled a lip at Chloe.

Chloe jabbed Muriel in the shoulder. "The chemistry just wasn't right between you. Don't worry, Mur. There'll be other men, men of real class." She stood and grabbed a handful of papers. "We'd better get these flyers out so people will know about this debate on Friday."

Chloe straightened her shoulders. "You've seen it on TV," she announced in her clear contralto to the crowded cafeteria. "You've read it on the news. It's not science fiction anymore. Come hear a debate on the ethics of cloning."

Chloe's beret went flying. The guy in a muscle shirt jammed it over his head and made a goofy face. "The ethics of clowning?" His friends whooped.

"Faber!" Chloe sneered at him and clucked. "Not clowning, you idiot. Cloning. You know, making copies of animals? Copies of people? Can you imagine a room full of Fabers?" Chloe widened her eyes at his buddies. "Scareee."

Faber's friends intoned, "Ooh, baaad." They elbowed him in the ribs. "She got you, Faber."

Faber's eyes narrowed at Chloe. "How 'bout a world full of maniac Mankewiczes?" He shuddered all over. "Arc, arc," he crowed.

Everyone laughed. Even Chloe. "Come to the debate Friday," she said to him, to all of them. "You might learn something."

Faber took the flyer she offered. As he turned to leave, he handed back her beret.

She held up a hand. "Keep it. It looks better on you."

He snorted and swaggered away.

"Genetic engineering," Chloe bellowed. "It's the ultimate power trip of man over beast. A total violation of animal rights. Who are we to mess around with natural evolution?"

She felt his presence before she saw him. Her scalp tingled. The faint scent of soap tickled her nose. She swallowed hard, and ended, "Who died and made us God?" She turned.

Brett met her eyes. "Good question," he said.

The air between them crackled. Silence stretched. He'd been avoiding her for more than a week now. She knew she'd have to face him sometime. Finally Chloe found her voice and said, "We're organizing a debate about cloning on Friday during lunch. The ethics, pro and con. Although there isn't anything to say in favor of it. Here." She handed him a flyer.

He stared at it for a moment before backing away. She noticed on his tray a hamburger and fries, the works. He met her eyes and said quietly, "You can't save the world, Chloe." Lowering his head, he turned and sauntered off.

"I can try!" she yelled after him. Her eyes welled with tears. *Oh, God,* she thought. *I'm going to lose it, right here in the cafeteria.*

"Chloe," Muriel called to her back.

Chloe swallowed the lump in her throat. Inhaling a shaky breath, she whirled back around. A group of people hovered around the ARC table.

"This is Tyler and Cam," Muriel said. "I didn't get everyone else's names."

Chloe scanned the group and saw a familiar face. "Alyssya?"

"Hi, Chloe," she said. "I was telling everyone about what you told me. You know, about killing baby animals for food, and all the other horrible things we do to animals. It's not right. We want to help. We want to join your club."

Chloe's jaw dropped. She looked at Muriel.

"I told them they'd have to talk to the president," she said.

Chloe counted five, six people. "Well, Mur," she replied. "Give them all membership forms."

Muriel blinked. Her lips curled in a smile as she rummaged through her bookbag. "Darn," she snapped her fingers, "I forgot the forms at home."

Chloe shrugged at the group. "You just can't get good help these days." She winked at Muriel. "I'll bring the membership forms tomorrow. Meanwhile, why don't you write down your names and phone numbers so we can let you know when the next meeting is."

Muriel shoved a notebook and mechanical pencil at Alyssya while Chloe considered the small group clustered around her table.

You're right, Brett, she thought. *I can't change the world. Not alone. But guess what? I'm not alone. There are others who care, and together we can—no, we will change the world.*